1775

Overlooked Heroines

Women Soldiers, Spies, and Humanitarians in the American Revolutionary War

By

Juanita Stellato Maldonado

Dorrance Publishing Co
585 Alpha Drive
Suite 103
Pittsburgh, PA 15238
Visit our website at *www.dorrancebookstore.com*

ISBN: 979-8-88925-193-4
eISBN: 979-8-88925-693-9

1775

Overlooked Heroines

Women Soldiers, Spies, and Humanitarians
in the American Revolutionary War

Contents

Introduction

The most well-known historical literature about the American Revolutionary War (1775-1783) describes valiant stories of "men" who fought on the battlefields as historical. However, seldomly are women included in these renowned books. When I say seldomly, I mean practically never. Case in point, I read *Scars of Independence* by Holger Hoock. He is a fantastic author; however, my issue is that he failed to mention the women who took part in the battles he wrote about, thus excluding them from history. Another book was *1776*, by David McCullough. Again, no mention of women soldiers. Yes, many historians write about Agent 355 or Deborah Sampson. However, what about the other women whose names are unknown throughout America? A historian's main job is to write down factual evidence and not to exclude anything even if it goes against their personal bias. A person researching a historical subject assumes the books they are studying have accurate descriptions of past events and the historian's interpretation of historical subjects to be true, and that genetic accounts of historical changes are fair and not misleading. Were these women's names left out purposely? Were they just overlooked? Did these famous authors decide that their heroic deeds were not brave? As a society, we should recreate the voice of the inaccurate past historical events and give life to those who are overlooked and viewed as inferior. Civilized societies still seem conditioned, educated, and brainwashed to think that women are second class and should not be moralized in daily life and in our history books. Or is it because most men do not want to see women as equal? There is a massive issue regarding gender inequality when writing women's history. Gender inequality Generally refers to the more excellent status and power of men over women that often emerges in controlling women's sexuality and other aspects of their behavior.[1]

This book's significance will validate the contributions of female soldiers, spies, and heroines who played a fundamental role in the Revolutionary War and provide evidence that they were not myths, as some male historians wish to claim. Moreover, confirmation will be submitted as evidence regarding these women's battles, espionage, and heroic adventures, along with their male names (new data) when enlisting in the Continental Army. The overall goal is to fill in the gaps of history and place these women back into the historical narrative, whose names are less celebrated and are overshadowed or misattributed simply because they are women, which is biased. Even though the women impersonating male soldiers might be few and far between during the Revolutionary War, they were still there. It was unusual and odd that a woman would be motivated to enlist in the Continental Army and volunteer to become spies and heroes. The question of how many females decided to enroll in the Continental Army during the Revolutionary War may never be resolved.

Whenever I did research, these brave women were noted in only a few books. They were often represented in a few sentences. Can you imagine a historian writing only three sentences about Milan (Cyrillic: Милан), Joan of Arc (Jehanne d'Arc), Diana, Princess of Wales, or even Wonder Woman (yes, she is a superhero, but you get the point)? Every little girl and boy should learn and be proud of knowing that ordinary women decided to fight against a mighty military force. The historical questions this book will answer are, did these women exist, what type of battles were they in, determine why women felt the need to physically fight in battles and abandon their social restraints, why did these women assume a soldier's role traditionally held by men, and how are they remembered in the twenty-first century. Since the beginning of time, women have abandoned their social restraints to fight as soldiers in any given war. Female soldiers in the Revolutionary War were not a new phenomenon. One great example was a warrior in the third-century (A.D. 226–248) Vietnam, Triệu Thị Trinh (or Triệu Thị Trinh). Trinh could no longer standby while the Chinese occupants were oppressing her and her people, so she took men into the mountains and trained them to be soldiers to fight against the Chinese. By the age of twenty-one, she fought over thirty battles against the Chinese and her rebel Army.[2] Another example is in the sixteenth century, the first female Queen Amina of Zaria (West Africa) personally led armies to expand the Zazzau empire.[3] This boosted her kingdom's wealth and power with gold, slaves, and new crops.[4]

Women, just like men, fought in the American Revolutionary War for many reasons. One, women had the same motivations as their male companions. Both genders shared a sense of pride when answering the call to fight for their country, knowing they played a small part in serving their community. Two, for better pay, soldiers were promised twenty-nine dollars per month, a small fortune for the time.[5] Three, to make a difference in the fight against tyranny. There is no gender distinction when it comes to patriotism. Even though women were forbidden to be active soldiers in the Continental Army, they still chose to join.[6] Historian Linda Grant De Pauw described in a 1981 journal article titled "Women in Combat: The Revolutionary War Experience" that during the American war for independence tens of thousands of women were involved in active combat. She divided them in three categories: First, many served in a distant branch of the Continental Army referred to as "women of the Army" (some may say these are camp followers); second, those enlisted as regular troops who fought in uniform with their male Continentals; and third, women serving in local militias.[7] Now isn't that amazing! This historian states thousands of women fought bravely on the battlefield; however, this is the only reference that I could locate stating this. No other notable history books share this historians research. None that I can find, anyway.

The battles, skirmishes, spies, and participation in the Revolutionary War yield a historiographical framework of male orientation. Historians concentrate on extraordinary male leadership while overemphasizing women's domestic responsibilities. The women in this book were daughters, wives, mothers, and sisters. Above all, these women were warriors. Women also served as spies during the Revolutionary War. The war was fought in the backyards of American families across the colonies and along the frontier. Women took an active role in alerting American troops to enemy movement, carried messages, and even transported contraband.[8] The women mentioned fought for liberty, authority, and the justification that citizens should rule over themselves rather than a monarchy. These names are less celebrated than they should be and are overshadowed by the Great Man Theory.

What is the Great Man Theory? Well, thanks for asking. Scottish essayist, historian, and philosopher Thomas Carlyle drafted this theory in 1840. The idea is that history can be primarily explained by the impact of great men or heroes.[9] Carlyle states that these men are born with the necessary attributes that set them apart from others and that these traits are responsible for their assuming positions of power and authority.[10] This theory was formulated when Carlyle analyzed the behaviors of military figures of the time. Once you finish this book, you will realize this theory is still being used. Women's historic involvement during the Revolutionary War is secluded, and most stories relate more to their domestic duties than their heroic deeds. They fought for future generations to live free within a society without tyranny imposed by an authoritarian monarchy. The central principle is that the legitimacy of the rule of law is based on the consent of the governed.[11]

The thinkers who formalized this concept are philosophers such as Thomas Hobbes and Jean-Jacques Rousseau. Liberty is an enlightenment idea reflected by citizens living freely without tyrannical restraints. Modern democracies/republics, in theory, are based on universal citizenship and enfranchisement for all adults, regardless of race, gender, or other classifications. Women are highly recognized in literature when it involves poetry, playwriters, romantic novels, domestic literature, civil rights, and cookbooks. However, what needs to be added is historical literature regarding females as soldiers. It is logical to conclude why these women were not written as soldiers; perhaps the reasoning is that before the twenty-first century, those roles were not open to women. Or is it because society or male historians did not feel the need to acknowledge the women mentioned in this book? You be the judge.

Physically the histories of women were largely underrepresented in history, and this has been an issue for five thousand years (since Herodotus of Halicarnassus (B.C. 484 – c. 425)), the proclaimed father of history. This is not a dead end; this book gives the opportunity to honor these women's experiences and how instrumental they were in assisting with securing America's freedom. Rosa Parks once said, "One person can change the world."[12]

Nevertheless, times are shifting; society is developing an interest in the story of women's history. Or are they? Scholars are convinced the second-wave feminist movement (1960s and 70s) created women's studies and therefore gave us our voice in the history books; however, while researching books published after the 1960s to current, there's still a small portion written about females' bravery. The majority of history is written about domestic duties that women partake in. That's pretty crappy in my view. The evidence presented in this book is significantly trustworthy and strictly authentic. The Revolutionary War was over 238 years ago, and there is no one alive to obtain an oral testimony to corroborate an event in history.

Literature Review

This section of the literature review will discuss the reoccurring theme discovered while conducting five years of research on this subject. Over one hundred books were purchased and reviewed. Many of these books were published in the late eighteen hundreds up until the twenty-first century. The reoccurring theme is that American women were excluded mainly in world-renowned publications regarding their heroic deeds. In the last half-century, historians finally started to pay attention to women in history (or so we thought) and have tried to modify historical records such as revisions on legends, myths, and literature created by men regarding the representation of women. However, America continues to see history through men's eyes.[13]

In the book *When We Dead Awaken: Writing as Re-Vision*, author Adrienne Rich asserts that re-vision—the act of looking back, of seeing with fresh eyes, of entering an old text from a new critical direction—is for women more than a chapter in cultural history: It is an act of survival.[14] In *The American Revolution* by John Fiske, volumes I and II, published in 1896, the author did not include any female soldiers, spies or even heroines in his books pertaining to the Revolutionary War.[15] In *1776* by David McCullough, published in 2005, the author recounts military campaigns during the Revolutionary War but leaves out the women who were involved in battles around New York. The book is mainly on the actions of Patriot generals.[16]

In *Great Women of the American Revolution* by Brianna Hall, published in 2013, the author only contributes four sentences to Emily Geiger, Ann Bates, Molly Pitcher, Margaret Corbin, Prudence Wright, Nancy Morgan Hart, and Elizabeth Bergen: women heroines of the American Revolutionary War (you will learn about them in later chapters).[17]

Activist and author Robin Morgan wrote in the 1970s that the women's liberation movement was creating history, or rather "herstory," coining the fashionable term that feminists used to emphasize the way in which women were consistently disregarded in historical narratives.[18] The teachings of women's involvement in American history still has much more for reevaluation and improvement. In the 1970s Robin noticed that women were excluded from American history and hoped that there would be change. In the year 2022 we still have the same problem!

One solution to this gap in history was to create women's studies in higher education, which made its debut in 1970. The first program was at San Diego State University.[19] In theory, women's studies teaches about women's social history, activities, and characteristics. However, not necessarily from any political or revisionist perspective; at the broadest, it implies a gender-based critique of all fields of academic inquiry and social endeavor.[20] When women are included in social studies texts, they are misrepresented and portrayed as occupying traditionally familiar gender roles. For example, while researching the women in this book, many of the women were described as myths and then spoke more in depth on their husbands' accomplishments versus the women themselves as individuals; most women were romanticized versus giving facts of their heroic deeds. One would assume that women's representation in history textbooks has increased since the 1970s. However, in 2017 the National Women's History Museum published a report on their findings on the status of women in the United States social studies standards. The museum analyzed the educational standards in social studies from grades K-12 in all fifty states, including Washington, D.C. The research concluded that since the 1960s, academic studies have found that women and minorities are vastly unrepresented in United States history textbooks. No kidding! Women continued to make up a small percentage of figures in U.S. history textbooks, including illustrations and sidebars.[21] According to *Smithsonian Magazine*'s review of the report, they calculated that 737 of specific historical figures are 559 men and 178 women, or approximately one woman for every three men are mentioned in the standards in place as of 2017.[22] That makes my blood boil. This demonstrates that the second-wave feminist movement and the push to have women's studies at universities has done absolutely nothing to increase women as heroes in publications relating to history or social studies.

When Americans recount the American Revolutionary War, the first thought that usually comes to mind is the "founding fathers." Books written throughout history mainly contribute to the generals of the Revolutionary War and founding fathers, like George Washington, Samuel Adams, John Adams, John Hancock, and those who signed the Declaration of Independence. This one-sided version of history requires adjustment. The failure of academia in correcting the continuous historical errors of excluding courageous women who fought one way or another during the American Revolutionary War; it reflects gender bias against women. My goal is that this book will educate and advocate for women to be incorporated in history as warriors, rather than history telling the story of their social class obligations and motherhood. We are more than just mothers.

CHAPTER 1
Events Leading Up to War

All civilized countries have their conception in stories, where a country shows equality to natives, which is always a myth, and we all know the conquer of a land writes a history that is factual and fiction, all merged into a good creation of a story. The creation of the United States is no exception. Every country has war; it seems like it is unavoidable. In both its modern and earliest manifestations, war centers on destroying the enemy's will or ability to resist by any means necessary, especially by attacks on civilian populations and infrastructures that support them.[23] The colonization of North America by Great Britain started in the sixteenth century. Eventually, it established thirteen colonies in North America (Connecticut, Delaware, Georgia, Maryland, Massachusetts, New Hampshire, New Jersey, New York, North Carolina, Pennsylvania, Rhode Island, South Carolina, and Virginia). The citizens of these colonies viewed themselves as British subjects and loyal to King George III of Great Britain and Ireland (1738-1820, ruled for almost sixty years). The British political system did not permit the colonies to be represented in Parliament (the governing body of the British government). When Parliament levied new taxes against the loyal British subjects, without representation, these colonialists turned their back on both king and country. The colonists argued that without representation in passing these acts that there should be no taxation. [24]

In 1765, the Declaratory Act was passed, which stated that the British Parliament had unlimited authority in the colonies. [25] Can you imagine if the United States President or the Prime Minister of England said that they had absolute power and authority over every individual in their country? That wouldn't go over too well. Hence, the Revolutionary War. The act also noted that the colonies were to be subordinate to and dependent upon the Imperial Crown, the Parliament of Great Britain, and the King's Majesty. This act gave the British political system full power and authority over the colonies. Colonists became sick and tired of obeying laws without a representative in Parliament and incurring revenue taxes passed by the British Parliament, which the colonists had no share in making. The acts bound the Colonists' hands to King George III, who ignored them until he desired their money to pay for the Seven-Years War (1756-1763). How very royal of him. For goodness' sake, King George never set foot in America. Actually, he hardly set foot in any of his kingdoms.

During the American Revolution, the population in North America was a little less than three million, of which half were slaves. Those who opposed imperialist Great Britain and King George III were Patriots, Rebels, or Whigs. Those who remained loyal to the British Crown were called Royalists, Loyalists, Tories, or King's Men. The Continental Army (formed on June 14, 1775) was comprised of Patriots, indentured servants, slaves, women, foreign allies to the Continental Army, and Indigenous people, who all played a crucial role in transforming Colonial America from imperialism into a republic nation. King George III underestimated the long war in North America. The thought of the British was that the rebellion of disobedient children would be over in a matter of days or weeks.

Many Americans assume King George was the main villain in the Revolutionary War. However, Parliament, Prime Minister Frederick North, and other ministers were the primary policymakers. You need to understand this correctly. The king dismissed the Whigs in favor of the Tories (two political powers in Britain). Could the reason be that Thomas Jefferson branded the king a plundering tyrant or that the Whigs in Parliament called the king an autocrat? Who knows the king's personal reasons? So, what is a Whig? Well, they opposed absolute monarchy and supported a system of government in which a monarch shares power with a constitutionally organized government. Tories were mostly upper-class men loyal to the Crown because they wanted to maintain their wealth. The Tories had no effective leadership and formed five governments over a six-year period. King George was a royal absolutist who believed that God gave him the right to rule any way he pleased. The Whigs, the architects of Salutary Neglect (Britain's unofficial policy, initiated by Prime Minister Robert Walpole, to relax the enforcement of strict regulations, particularly trade laws, imposed on the American colonies late in the seventeenth and early in the eighteenth centuries), supported a hands-off approach that saw the colonies thrive, but that was not enough for Great Britain. Parliament and the king wanted complete control.

HERE is one of the main reasons why the war happened. Pay attention, kids. Judicially the colonies were not given the right that other British citizens had when it came to the judicial process in the colonies. Instead, those on trial were forced to travel to Britain to hear their cases. How long was the voyage, you wonder? Well, it took an estimated 25 to 30 days from the English Channel to the coast of America, roughly 3,000 nautical miles. The British empire functioned successfully with all its territories because of a willingness (forced willingness) on both sides of the Atlantic to avoid problematic constitutional concerns. There needed to be a clear and compelling historical pattern based on British Constitutional history by which the colonists could be integrated into the British empire, meaning that royal subjects living in Colonial and other British territories were not distinguished as true British subjects and therefore were excluded from the British Constitution, but not British laws and taxation. Yeah, seems fair, just kidding. That was how, in Britain's mind, they were able to pass all these laws and taxes without violating the British Constitution. The American War of Independence began with the first military conflict, Lexington, Massachusetts (April 19, 1775), known as the battles of Lexington and Concord. The last battle was 608.5 miles away in the last military battle in Yorktown, Virginia (September 28 – October 19, 1781).

In August 1775, Richard Penn and Arthur Lee arrived in England carrying Congress' petition (a.k.a. the olive branch). This was a final effort by the colonists to prevent war with Britain. The American diplomats presented the petition to William Legge, 2nd Earl of Dartmouth, who attempted to deliver it to the king and, well, he refused to read it.

Olive Branch from the Colonies

To the king's most excellent Majesty: Most gracious sovereign,
We, your Majesty's faithful subjects of the colonies of new

Hampshire, Massachusetts bay, Rhode island and Providence Plantations, Connecticut, New York, New Jersey, Pennsylvania, the counties of New Castle, Kent, and Sussex, on Delaware, Maryland, Virginia, North Carolina, and South Carolina, in behalf of ourselves, and the inhabitants of these colonies, who have deputed us to represent them in General Congress, entreat your Majesty's gracious attention to this our humble petition.

The union between our Mother country and these colonies, and the energy of mild and just government, produced benefits so remarkably important, and afforded such an assurance of their permanency and increase, that the wonder and envy of other Nations were excited, while they beheld Great Britain riseing to a power the most extraordinary the world had ever known.

Her rivals, observing that there was no probability of this happy connexion being broken by civil dissensions, and apprehending its future effects, if left any longer undisturbed, resolved to prevent her receiving such continual and formidable accessions of wealth and strength, by checking the growth of these settlements from which they were to be derived.

In the prosecution of this attempt, events so unfavourable to the design took place, that every friend to the interests of Great Britain and these colonies, entertained pleasing and reasonable expectations of seeing an additional force and extention immediately given to the operations of the union hitherto experienced, by an enlargement of the dominions of the Crown, and the removal of ancient and warlike enemies to a greater distance.

At the conclusion, therefore, of the late war, the most glorious and advantageous that ever had been carried on by British arms, your loyal colonists having contributed to its success, by such repeated and strenuous exertions, as frequently procured them the distinguished approbation of your Majesty, of the late king, and of Parliament, doubted not but that they should be permitted, with the rest of the empire, to share in the blessings of peace, and the emoluments of vic tory and conquest. While these recent and honorable acknowledg ments of their merits remained on record in the journals and acts of that august legislature, the Parliament, undefaced by the imputation or even the suspicion of any offence, they were alarmed by a new system of statutes and regulations adopted for the administration of the colonies, that filled their minds with the most painful fears and jealousies; and, to their inexpressible astonishment, perceived the dangers of a foreign quarrel quickly succeeded by domestic dangers, in their judgment, of a more dreadful kind.

Nor were their anxieties alleviated by any tendency in this system to promote the welfare of the Mother country. For tho' its effects were more immediately felt by them, yet its influence appeared to be injurious to the commerce and prosperity of Great Britain.

We shall decline the ungrateful task of describing the irksome variety of artifices, practised by many of your Majesty's Ministers, the delusive pretences, fruitless terrors, and unavailing severities, that have, from time to time, been dealt out by them, in their attempts to execute this impolitic plan, or of traceing, thro' a series of years past, the progress of the unhappy differences between Great Britain and these colonies, which have flowed from this fatal source.

Your Majesty's Ministers, persevering in their measures, and proceeding to open hostilities for enforcing them, have compelled us to arm in our own defence, and have engaged us in a controversy so peculiarly abhorrent to the affections of your still faithful colonists, that when we consider whom we must oppose in this contest, and if it continues, what may be the consequences, our own particular misfor tunes are accounted by us only as parts of our distress.

Knowing to what violent resentments and incurable animosities, civil discords are apt to exasperate and inflame the contending parties, we think ourselves required by indispensable obligations to Almighty God, to your Majesty, to our fellow subjects, and to ourselves, immediately to use all the means in our power, not incompatible with our safety, for stopping the further effusion of blood, and for averting the impending calamities that threaten the British Empire.

Thus called upon to address your Majesty on affairs of such moment to America, and probably to all your dominions, we are earnestly desirous of performing this office, with the utmost deference for your Majesty; and we therefore pray, that your royal magnanimity and benevolence may make the most favourable construction of our expressions on so uncommon an occasion. Could we represent in their full force, the sentiments that agitate the minds of us your dutiful subjects, we are persuaded your Majesty would ascribe any seeming deviation from reverence in our language, and even in our conduct, not to any reprehensible intention, but to the impossibility of reconciling the usual appearances of respect, with a just attention to our own preservation against those artful and cruel enemies, who abuse your royal confidence and authority, for the purpose of effecting our destruction.

Attached to your Majesty's person, family, and government, with all devotion that principle and affection can inspire, connected with Great Britain by the strongest ties that can unite societies, and deploring every event that tends in any degree to weaken them, we solemnly assure your Majesty, that we not only most ardently desire the former harmony between her and these colonies may be restored, but that a concord may be established between them upon so firm a basis as to perpetuate its blessings, uninterrupted by any future dissentions, to succeeding generations in both countries, and to transmit your Majesty's Name to posterity, adorned with that signal and lasting glory, that has attended the memory of those illustrious personages, whose virtues and abilities have extricated states from dangerous convulsions, and, by securing happiness to others, have erected the most noble and durable monuments to their own fame.

We beg leave further to assure your Majesty, that notwithstanding the sufferings of your loyal colonists, during the course of the present controversy, our breasts retain too tender a regard for the kingdom from which we derive our origin, to request such a reconciliation as might in any manner be inconsistent with her dignity or her welfare. These, related as we are to her, honor and duty, as well as inclination, induce us to support and advance; and the apprehensions that now oppress our hearts with unspeakable grief, being once removed, your Majesty will find your faithful subjects on this continent ready and willing at all times, as they ever have been, with their lives and fortunes, to assert and maintain the rights and interests of your Majesty, and of our Mother country.

We, therefore, beseech your Majesty, that your royal authority and influence may be graciously interposed to procure us relief from our afflicting fears and jealousies, occasioned by the system before men tioned, and to settle peace through every part of your dominions, with all humility submitting to your Majesty's wise consideration whether it may not be expedient for facilitating those important purposes, that your Majesty be pleased to direct some mode, by which the united applications of your faithful colonists to the throne, in pursuance of their common councils, may be improved into a happy and permanent reconciliation; and that, in the mean time, measures may be taken for preventing the further destruction of the lives of your Majesty's subjects; and that such statutes as more immediately distress any of your Majesty's colonies may be repealed.

> *For by such arrangements as your Majesty's wisdom can form, for collecting the united sense of your American people, we are convinced your Majesty would receive such satisfactory proofs of the disposition of the colonists toward their sovereign and parent state, that the wished for opportunity would soon be restored to them, of evincing the sincerity of their professions, by every testimony of devotion becoming the most dutiful subjects, and the most affectionate colonists.*
>
> *That your Majesty may enjoy a long and prosperous reign, and that your descendants may govern your dominions with honor to them selves and happiness to their subjects, is our sincere and fervent prayer.*

This extremely long petition could have been summed up in a few sentences. For example, if I were writing it, I would simply say: "Your majesty views the colonies in North America as British subjects. However, you do not grant the colonies representation in Parliament per the British Constitution. And since we are British citizens, the Constitution applies to us. If you consider giving us representation in Parliament, these skirmishes might cease." Something to that effect. I would not have three pages of kissing his royal behind and asking him to be respectful to his citizens. Come on, with the history of Great Britain conquering other countries and how they treated the inhabitants, did they honestly think that the king and Parliament would be kind to their territories? I think not.

In 1775, the king addressed the House of Lords and the House of Commons regarding the rebellion in the colonies. In his speech, the king consented to dispatch British troops to squash this traitor's rebellion. Giving in to the demands of the colonies would only show weakness, or so the king thought. On August 23, 1775, the Proclamation for Suppressing Rebellion and Sedition (Proclamation of Rebellion) was enacted. This declared that the American colonies were open in an avowed rebellion. Before the British Empire formally declared war on the colonies, there were at least thirteen recorded battles. [26]

Proclamation of Rebellion

Whereas many of our subjects in divers parts of our Colonies and Plantations in North America, misled by dangerous and ill designing men, and forgetting the allegiance which they owe to the power that has protected and supported them; after various disorderly acts committed in disturbance of the publick peace, to the obstruction of lawful commerce, and to the oppression of our loyal subjects carrying on the same; have at length proceeded to open and avowed rebellion, by arraying themselves in a hostile manner, to withstand the execution of the law, and traitorously preparing, ordering and levying war against us: And whereas, there is reason to apprehend that such rebellion hath been much promoted and encouraged by the traitorous correspondence, counsels and comfort of divers wicked and desperate persons within this Realm:

To the end therefore, that none of our subjects may neglect or violate their duty through ignorance thereof, or through any doubt of the protection which the law will afford to their loyalty and zeal, we have thought fit, by and with the advice of our Privy Council, to issue our Royal Proclamation, hereby declaring, that not only all our Officers, civil and military, are obliged to exert their utmost endeavours to suppress such rebellion, and to bring the traitors to justice, but that all our subjects of this Realm, and the dominions thereunto belonging, are bound by law to be aiding and assisting in the suppression of such rebellion, and to disclose and make known all traitorous conspiracies and attempts against us, our crown and dignity; and we do accordingly strictly charge and command all our Officers, as well civil as military, and all others our obedient and loyal subjects, to use their utmost endeavours to withstand and suppress such rebellion, and to disclose and make known all treasons and traitorous conspiracies which they shall know to be against us, our crown and dignity; and for that purpose, that they transmit to one of our principal Secretaries of State, or other proper officer, due and full information of all persons who shall be found carrying on correspondence with, or in any manner or degree aiding or abetting the persons now in open arms and rebellion against our Government, within any of our Colonies and Plantations in North America, in order to bring to condign punishment the authors, perpetrators, and abetters of such traitorous designs.

Given at our Court at St. James's the twenty-third day of August, one thousand seven hundred and seventy-five, in the fifteenth year of our reign.

GOD save the KING.

The American Revolutionary War officially ended with Great Britain on September 3, 1783, after Benjamin Franklin, John Jay, and John Adams negotiated a peace treaty with representatives of the king in Paris.[27] Based on a 1782 preliminary Treaty of Paris, the agreement recognized the United States' independence. The 1783 Treaty was a series of treaties that established peace between Great Britain and the allied nations of France, Netherlands, and Spain.[28] At the time of the American Revolutionary War, Britain was also involved in a World War. Their navy was spread thin across three continents. The British Constitution did not govern over the English colonists. Historian Charles McIlwain argued the constitutional problem lies with Britain's Parliamentary system, which was unsuitable to govern territories.[29] America and Britain did not want to publicly acknowledge that both countries were in a political conflict. The British responded by adopting an assertion of power without considering the reaction from the colonies. It is essential to understand that the British Constitution (at that time) stated that no British citizen would be forced to pay a tax when not agreed upon through representation in Parliament. Lords, governors, and judges in North America were appointed and controlled by the Crown and spoke for the interests of the king versus the subjects (colonists) living in North American territories. Their salaries were paid by the Crown rather than by

Colonial legislators. British PM (Prime Minister) George Grenville and Thomas Whately attempted to justify the Colonists' absence of representation in Colonial taxation by developing a theory called "Virtual Representation" that the colonists were virtually represented in Parliament. Parliament accepted this theory as law and passed several acts to raise revenue in North America. Say what, so a theory can be law? Got it! Parliament rejected any criticism that virtual representation was constitutionally invalid as a whole. See their kids, they passed unlawful taxes on the colonies. They knew it was wrong. Did they care? No! Britain placed a financial burden on the colonies by demanding them to pay in taxes for the cost of their current defenses, the French and Indian War (1754–1763, estimated debt £140,000,000), and the War with Spain (1585-1604, estimated debt £4,500,000). Hence, the countdown to the Revolutionary War.

The way Britain kept their economy thriving was through a method called mercantilism. The British restricted how the colonies spent their money to control North America's economy. The British held what goods the colonies could produce, what ships to use, and whom they could conduct trade with. The colonies were the suppliers of raw materials such as lumber, rice, cotton, tobacco, furs, beaver pelts, and dried fish to Great Britain. There were several acts (taxes and laws) levied on the colonists. It was only a matter of time until they were overwhelmed with being overtaxed. Hence the decision to fight against tyranny became a viable option. Countdown to War begins with a few acts. These acts violated the guaranteed Rights of Englishmen. Since they were British subjects, they fell under the protection of British laws; according to the Rights of Englishmen law, Englishmen were to have a representative in Parliament. Did that happen to the Americans? Not at all. This example demonstrates that Great Britain did not function as a democracy; the government treated the colonists differently than those within the island of Great Britain's borders.

The most destructive taxes the colonies had to endure (but not all of them). Let's start with the Quartering Act of 1765, which required Colonial assemblies to house and supply British soldiers without the homeowner's consent. Many colonists objected to providing housing and supplies to the British soldiers. Several Colonial assemblies refused to vote for the mandated supplies. The New York assembly refused, and as a lesson Britain disbanded the New York assembly in

1767. Other assemblies resented this retaliation and feared their assembly could be shut down. This is why the Third Amendment to the U.S. Constitution was created. No soldier shall, in a time of peace, be quartered in any house, without the consent of the owner, nor in the time of war, but in a manner to be prescribed by law.

The Stamp Act (1765) was a tax on all printed materials; each page of a book, newspaper, playing cards, and even dice was stamped on each side. And each stamp was a cost. The General voice throughout the colonies was that business shall go on as if the act had not passed and ignored the new tax. The Colonist became enraged and reacted to the Stamp Act by protesting, intimidating stamp collectors into resigning, and resorting to mob violence in the streets of New York with a banner saying *The Folly of England, the Ruin of America*. The Stamp Act was an attempt to raise money in the colonies without the approval of Colonial legislatures.[30] Great Britain generated over £100,000 in tax revenue with very little in collection expenses. However, Parliament accepted defeat and repealed the Stamp Act of 1766. Many in the Parliament were hesitant to rescind the Stamp Act. They believed it would send a message that all people had to do was protest and riot to get their way. Nonetheless, the act was repealed.

The Tea Act of 1773 was to basically bail out the troubled British East India Company. So, this tax was not meant to increase the revenue of Great Britain. It was meant to increase the revenue of the East India Company. The British government granted the company a monopoly on importing and selling tea in the colonies. The colonists had never accepted the constitutionality of the duty on tea, and the Tea Act rekindled their opposition to it.[31] Americans should understand that tea to the British subjects was like America's addiction to coffee. Or better yet, America's obsession with Starbucks. Now you get it. The Tea Act was passed in May. So, in December 1773, American colonists in Boston formed a group called the Boston Tea Party. I wonder if Americans would form an angry mob if all the Starbucks closed. That might be entertaining to watch. The Boston Tea Party boarded three tea ships docked at Griffin's Wharf and dumped the tea into the harbor. The Boston Tea Party was organized by the Sons of Liberty, a secret organization created to advance the rights of the European colonists. Some famous members were Oliver Wolcott (signer of the Articles of Confederation and the Declaration of Independence), Marinus Willett (Lieutenant Colonel in the independence war), John Hancock, and Samuel Adams, to name a few. An estimated three hundred and forty-two chests of tea went into Boston harbor (valued at £18,000, which is about $1 million in today's money). New York and other ports around the colonies also protested against this act. The British government took this as an act of defiance.

The Declaratory Act of 1766, also known as the American Colonies Act, accompanied the repeal of the Stamp Act, which stated that the British government had free and total legislative power over the colonies. Was Parliament intentionally trying to upset the thirteen colonies, or were they, like today's politicians, oblivious to what their people wanted? Nope, Parliament did not care about how these laws affected their subjects. The Declaratory Act proclaimed three main things:

1. The Colonial assemblies did not have the sole and exclusive right of imposing duties and taxes upon their Colonial subjects.
2. Parliament had full power and authority to make laws and statutes of sufficient force and validity to bind the colonies and people of America[32] in all cases whatsoever, just as it had in Britain.
3. Any laws or resolutions made by the Colonial assemblies denying Parliament's rightful authority to make laws governing them were repealed and made utterly null and void.

So instead of passing laws based on the Virtual Representation theory, they passed a law that made it clear that Great Britain and Parliament had full authority to make laws and statutes a significant force that bound the colonies' subjects of the Crown. However, the colonists still were not represented in Parliament per the British constitution. In 1767, Parliament passed the Townshend Act, which was intended to regulate Colonial trade on paper, paints, glass, and tea, as well as goods imported into the colonies from Great Britain. The Townshend Act was named after a British Chancellor of the Exchequer named Charles Townshend. The additions to this act intended to refashion the Colonial governments. Those additions permitted British officials to search colonists' homes and businesses, develop new courts without a jury to prosecute smugglers, and establish the American Customs Board to enforce trade and collect taxes for the British empire. This would become a fatal experiment with forcing taxation onto the colonies by Parliament thousands of miles away and whose king never set foot on American soil. *The 4th Amendment of U.S. Constitution protects American citizens from unreasonable searches and seizures.*

In 1770 the Townshend Act was repealed, except for the tax on tea. Britain added more fuel to the fire when, in 1773, they introduced the Tea Act. The British government argued that tea was not grown in England and thus the tariff would not injure British merchants. Benjamin Franklin had informed the British Parliament that the colonies intended to start manufacturing their own goods rather than paying duties on imports.[33] The Colonists protested against non-importation of British goods. The act's primary purpose was not to raise revenue from the colonies but to bail out East India Company, which was close to bankruptcy. East India Company was a critical factor in the British economy.[34] This act gave the East India Company a monopoly on British tea, meaning it had full control over all tea sold in North America. Even though the cost of tea was reduced, the colonists were furious because they were compelled to purchase only the British East India Company's tea and no longer had the option of purchasing the tea they preferred.

The slogan "No taxation without representation" appeared for the first time in a headline of a magazine article printed in 1768.

The Intolerable (Coercive) Act in 1774 was established in response to non-importation and to punish those colonists who participated in the after years of unpopular laws, being unrepresented in Parliament, and being forced to pay taxes. The thirteen colonies were fed up and furious and unanimously declared separation and independence from an imperial government. The Declaration of Independence listed twenty-seven complaints/grievances from the thirteen colonies.[35] (signed by 56 congressional delegates). In all the history books I've read about American history, not one adds the entire text of the Declaration of Independence. Yes, it is long; however, it is necessary for the reader to understand why it was written. Below is the text from the Declaration of Independence—I was hesitant in adding it. However, I realized that many Americans still have yet to read it. So, now's your chance. Who knows, this might revive a passion of love for this country. Here we go:

In Congress, July 4, 1776

The unanimous Declaration of the thirteen United States of America, When in the Course of human events, it becomes necessary for one people to dissolve the political bands which have connected them with another, and to assume among the powers of the earth, the separate and equal station to which the Laws of Nature and of Nature's God entitle them, a decent respect to the opinions of mankind requires that they should declare the causes which impel them to the separation.

We hold these truths to be self-evident, that all men are created equal, that they are endowed by their Creator with certain unalienable Rights, that among these are Life, Liberty and the pursuit of Happiness.—That to secure these rights, Governments are instituted among Men, deriving their just powers from the consent of the governed, —That whenever any Form of Government becomes destructive of these ends, it is the Right of the People to alter or to abolish it, and to institute new Government, laying its foundation on such principles and organizing its powers in such form, as to them shall seem most likely to effect their Safety and Happiness. Prudence, indeed, will dictate that Governments long established should not be changed for light and transient causes; and accordingly all experience hath shewn, that mankind are more disposed to suffer, while evils are sufferable, than to right themselves by abolishing the forms to which they are accustomed. But when a long train of abuses and usurpations, pursuing invariably the same Object evinces a design to reduce them under absolute Despotism, it is their right, it is their duty, to throw off such Government, and to provide new Guards for their future security.—Such has been the patient sufferance of these Colonies; and such is now the necessity which constrains them to alter their former Systems of Government. The history of the present King of Great Britain is a history of repeated injuries and usurpations, all having in direct object the establishment of an absolute Tyranny over these States. To prove this, let Facts be submitted to a candid world.

He has refused his Assent to Laws, the most wholesome and necessary for the public good.

He has forbidden his Governors to pass Laws of immediate and pressing importance, unless suspended in their operation till his Assent should be obtained; and when so suspended, he has utterly neglected to attend to them.

He has refused to pass other Laws for the accommodation of large districts of people, unless those people would relinquish the right of Representation in the Legislature, a right inestimable to them and formidable to tyrants only.

He has called together legislative bodies at places unusual, uncomfortable, and distant from the depository of their public Records, for the sole purpose of fatiguing them into compliance with his measures.

He has dissolved Representative Houses repeatedly, for opposing with manly firmness his invasions on the rights of the people.

He has refused for a long time, after such dissolutions, to cause others to be elected; whereby the Legislative powers, incapable of Annihilation, have returned to the People at large for their exercise; the State remaining in the mean time exposed to all the dangers of invasion from without, and convulsions within.

He has endeavoured to prevent the population of these States; for that purpose obstructing the Laws for Naturalization of Foreigners; refusing to pass others to encourage their migrations hither, and raising the conditions of new Appropriations of Lands.

He has obstructed the Administration of Justice, by refusing his Assent to Laws for establishing Judiciary powers.

He has made Judges dependent on his Will alone, for the tenure of their offices, and the amount and payment of their salaries.

He has erected a multitude of New Offices, and sent hither swarms of Officers to harrass our people, and eat out their substance.

He has kept among us, in times of peace, Standing Armies without the Consent of our legislatures.

He has affected to render the Military independent of and superior to the Civil power.

He has combined with others to subject us to a jurisdiction foreign to our constitution, and unacknowledged by our laws; giving his Assent to their Acts of pretended Legislation:

For Quartering large bodies of armed troops among us:

For protecting them, by a mock Trial, from punishment for any Murders which they should commit on the Inhabitants of these States:

For cutting off our Trade with all parts of the world:

For imposing Taxes on us without our Consent:

For depriving us in many cases, of the benefits of Trial by Jury:

For transporting us beyond Seas to be tried for pretended offences

For abolishing the free System of English Laws in a neighbouring Province, establishing therein an Arbitrary government, and enlarging its Boundaries so as to render it at once an example and fit instrument for introducing the same absolute rule into these Colonies:

For taking away our Charters, abolishing our most valuable Laws, and altering fundamentally the Forms of our Governments:

For suspending our own Legislatures, and declaring themselves invested with power to legislate for us in all cases whatsoever.

He has abdicated Government here, by declaring us out of his Protection and waging War against us.

He has plundered our seas, ravaged our Coasts, burnt our towns, and destroyed the lives of our people.

He is at this time transporting large Armies of foreign Mercenaries to compleat the works of death, desolation and tyranny, already begun with circumstances of Cruelty & perfidy scarcely paralleled in the most barbarous ages, and totally unworthy the Head of a civilized nation.

He has constrained our fellow Citizens taken Captive on the high Seas to bear Arms against their Country, to become the executioners of their friends and Brethren, or to fall themselves by their Hands.

He has excited domestic insurrections amongst us, and has endeavoured to bring on the inhabitants of our frontiers, the merciless Indian Savages, whose known rule of warfare, is an undistinguished destruction of all ages, sexes and conditions.

In every stage of these Oppressions We have Petitioned for Redress in the most humble terms: Our repeated Petitions have been answered only by repeated injury. A Prince whose character is thus marked by every act which may define a Tyrant, is unfit to be the ruler of a free people.

Nor have We been wanting in attentions to our Brittish brethren. We have warned them from time to time of attempts by their legislature to extend an unwarrantable jurisdiction over us. We have reminded them of the circumstances of our emigration and settlement here. We have appealed to their native justice and magnanimity, and we have conjured them by the ties of our common kindred to disavow these usurpations, which, would inevitably interrupt our connections and correspondence. They too have been deaf to the voice of justice and of consanguinity. We must, therefore, acquiesce in the necessity, which denounces our Separation, and hold them, as we hold the rest of mankind, Enemies in War, in Peace Friends.

We, therefore, the Representatives of the united States of America, in General Congress, Assembled, appealing to the Supreme Judge of the world for the rectitude of our intentions, do, in the Name, and by Authority of the good People of these Colonies, solemnly publish and declare, That these United Colonies are, and of Right ought to be Free and Independent States; that they are Absolved from all Allegiance to the British Crown, and that all political connection between them and the State of Great Britain, is and ought to be totally dissolved; and that as Free and Independent States, they have full Power to levy War, conclude Peace, contract Alliances, establish Commerce, and to do all other Acts and Things which Independent States may of right do. And for the support of this Declaration, with a firm reliance on the protection of divine Providence, we mutually pledge to each other our Lives, our Fortunes and our sacred Honor.

Five of the 56 men who signed the Declaration of Independence were captured by the British tortured and put to death, twelve had their homes burned to the ground. By signing this document each man understood that this was high treason against the King of England. They were signing their death warrants. John Hancock and John Adams were hunted by British General Thomas Gage. Francis Lewis had his home and properties destroyed. The enemy jailed his wife, and she died within a few months. John Hart was driven from his wife's bedside as she was dying. Their thirteen children fled for their lives. His fields and his gristmill were laid to waste. For more than a year he lived in forests and caves, returning home to find his wife dead and his children vanished. A few weeks later he died from exhaustion and a broken heart. Norris and Livingston suffered similar fates.[36] While writing this book, I sometimes reflected that if we had to declare independence from a king in today's America, would we still have patriotic Americans that would stand up and say yes, no matter the cost? Or did cancel culture, which policed and punished those who practiced their First Amendment rights, along with political correctness, indeed destroy Patriotism? Only time will tell.

Those who opposed Great Britain were called Patriots and those who remained loyal to the British government and Crown were called Loyalists and Tories. The Continental Army, Patriot militias, free Africans, indentured servants, women, and slaves all played a role in transforming American into, in theory, a free republic. King George III called the Revolutionary War a rebellion because his rebellious children defied their father. Before the battle of Lexington and Concord (April 1775), the uprising was nonviolent to a certain degree. The British troops tormented colonists, raped women, beat the poor, hung children for stealing food, and burned farms all because they could. And let me also state the Patriot militia was not as innocent as everyone thinks. They also harassed Loyalists and Tories by stealing and burning down farms and houses. There is a wonderful book titled *Scars of Independence* by Holger Hoock that gives great detail of what the Tories and the Patriots did to one another in the war. The British opened fire on their fellow citizens first in Boston (Boston Massacre, 1770). The Revolutionary War was not fought because of economics, or to put the founding fathers in charge; it was to stop the brutality in which the British troops put upon those who lived in the thirteen united colonies. The issue with economics came after the war. It is true that the American Revolutionary War was run by the ruling class. However, we need those with higher education to conduct diplomatic relations. I understand why the ruling class was in charge. The critical point in leaving a dictatorship is that the founding fathers wanted a government ruled by *the people, for the people,* instead of ruled by a monarchy. What does this mean? Glad you asked. It means *"that these dead shall not have died in vain—that this nation, under God, shall have a new birth of freedom and that government of the people, by the people, for the people, shall not perish from the earth"* (U.S. President Abraham Lincoln, The Gettysburg Address, November 19, 1863). This was to have a say in their government through representatives they elected and that the people would make the laws that would, in theory, protect the citizens of this country. From reading this book you understand that Parliament did not care about the colonies; if they did, Parliament would have permitted them to be represented. If Parliament had compassion, perhaps there would not have been a war. The keyword there is *perhaps.*

Since the first King of Britain (Egbert A.D. 827-839, first monarch to have extensive rule over all of Anglo-Saxon England), Britain has had a long history of slaughtering those who stood up against the monarchy. Throughout Great Britain's existence, the country has invaded and conquered nine out of ten of the world's nations.[37] At Britain's pivotal point, the empire expanded around twenty-five percent of the world's total landmass (Africa, America, Asia, and Australia). Today Britain retains sovereignty over fourteen external countries. By 1770, there was an estimated one thousand British troops occupying Boston, Massachusetts, with an estimated population of 15,000 or 16,000 depending on which historian is writing the book. Bostonians had to compete with these British soldiers when it came to jobs, housing, and several clashes between British soldiers and Patriots occurred. Tensions were high with British troops fighting the colonists and Bostonians fighting against each other (Tories vs. Patriots). This just added more fuel to the fire to those who thought they were being treated unfairly.

Lord Hillsborough, Secretary of State for the colonies,[38] dispatched two regiments equaling to 4,000 additional troops joining the thousands already there to restore order in Boston, (imperial order) to gain control over the colonists who were protesting and who were the non-importation the Townshend Act. However, sending more troops created a volatile environment for everyone in Boston. Britain thought because they were superior in manpower, naval, and military technology (of that time) that they would easily defeat the colonists. The British troops did not adapt to guerrilla warfare during the Revolutionary War. Their tactics were ignorant because they did not study the enemy nor the terrain; they relied upon Indigenous tribes to assist them to navigate British troops through the country. England lost to America during the Revolutionary War because of their arrogance. Yup, I said it. The British empire pursued a desire to win the war versus the illogical strategic goal of winning over the people they wished to rule over. They failed to recognize that you will not win the war if you do not win over the people.

The British did not follow rule number three of Sun Tzu's *Art of War* (published roughly 5th century B.C.). Know yourself, know the enemy. The Revolution's stories of its battles can hardly be told regarding long-term strategies and its success or failure. Neither side ever had any consistent plan to conduct the war. After the British lost the battle of Saratoga (1777), the British Army turned its attention toward the South. They devised a Southern Strategy expecting support from Loyalists living in the South. Several key factors contributed to Britain's unsuccessful attempt at its Southern Strategy. Factor one: The British had two assumptions. First, the British thought there were many Loyalists in the South. Moreover, the British assumed these wealthy Loyalists would be willing to fight in a militia. This was a critical miscalculation because neither General Sir Henry Clinton nor General Charles Cornwallis had the means to raise resources for training and equipping the Loyalists with weapons. Most of the time, the British, who retained the strategic initiative, failed to use it to great advantage. They were highly uncertain about their objective; they made plans from year to year and seldom coordinated them even for a single year. Blame for this hesitant approach falls in almost equal part on the administration in England and the British commanders in America. King George III; Lord Frederick North (Prime Minister of Britain), his Principal Minister; and Lord George Germain, Secretary of State for the American Department, were the three British officials mainly responsible for the war's conduct. In assessing blame in this fashion, one must keep in mind the difficulties of logistics and communications under which the British labored. These difficulties made it virtually impossible to coordinate plans over great distances or assemble men and materials in time to pursue one logical and consistent strategy.

The American strategy was primarily defensive and consequently had to be mainly shaped to counter British moves.[39] Uncertainties about the supply of both men and materials acted on the American side even more effectively to thwart a consistent plan for winning the war. If it were not for the assistance of France in the Revolutionary War, America might have remained under British control. France was the enemy of Great Britain and lost a lot of land to them during the Treaty of Paris (1763). France was not just being nice in helping America; after the treaty was signed, France was planning on war with Britain, and this was too great of an opportunity to pass up. France got involved because they assumed that when America won, America would give back their land in North America. Well, that did not happen. However, in 1778 America and France signed a treaty (The Franco-American) alliance, which promised mutual military support in case another war happened again. During the Revolutionary War, France provided the colonies with modern weaponry and assisted America with their pocketbook.[40] Without the assistance of France, perhaps the colonists would have lost. We could only assume a different outcome if France decided not to enter the war and side with America.

Spain also came to the aid of the Americans in their time of need.[41] Like France, Spain was motivated to help the colonists because they wanted to regain the land that they had lost from the British empire. However, many historians would disagree with my assessment. Spain also signed the Treaty of Paris, which they lost land to Britain. Oh, and let's not forget about the Dutch, even though they tried to remain neutral only because the British fleet was more superior than the Dutch Republic.[42] So the Dutch Republic's involvement was trading war material for both sides. War makes men rich.

FRANCE	SPAIN	DUTCH
Weapons	Weapons	War materials
Soldiers	Ammunition	Funding
Funding	Funding	
Gunpowder	Naval support	
Naval support		

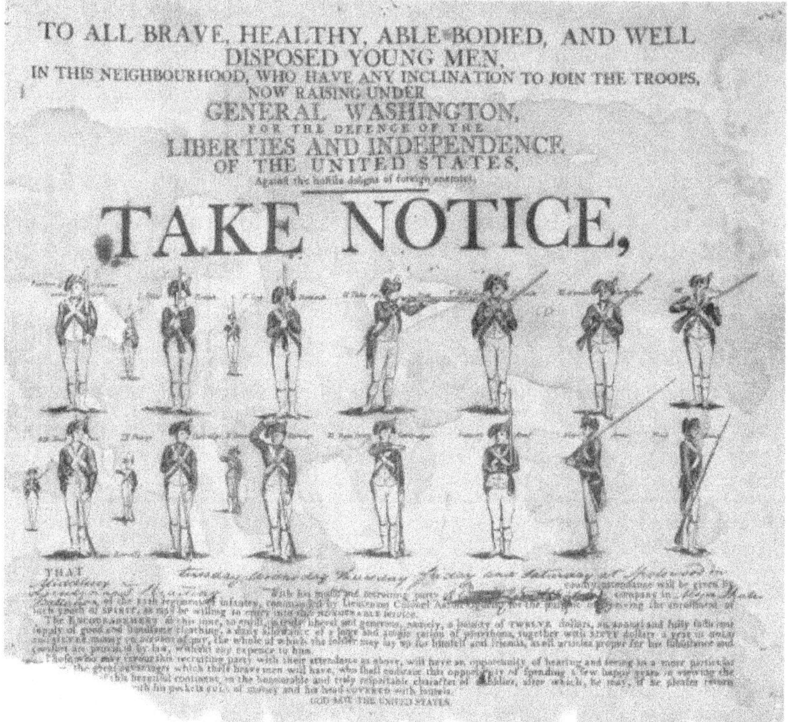

Source: Broadside soliciting recruits for the Continental Army, ca. 1775
Connecticut Historical Society

Ordinary people found the courage to fight against tyranny, to defend their property, which makes them extraordinary. Many were forced to fight in the American Revolutionary War. Sometimes ordinary people run away from war or conflict; however, you cannot outrun a war when it is in your own backyard. Many colonialists thought it was better to put their heads in the sand and ignore what was happening around them (many were on the fence). Colonists were fighting to end oppression by a monarchy that ruled them with an iron fist, who lived thousands of miles away and, by the way, King George III never set foot on American soil. Extraordinary people had to break their social constraints to fight for freedom.

"What monarchs and dictators fail to recognize, is that Patriotism,
once ignited, cannot be stomped out, even with their last dying breath."
- Juanita Stellato Maldonado

CHAPTER 2
Breaking the Rules of Social Convention

In general, eighteenth-century prospective texts argued that men and women were naturally different, and that these differences not only shaped their characters but suited each sex to specific activities and roles in society.[43] Women in Colonial America and England were responsible for managing the household, tending to the farm, appeasing their husband, and cooking. Even though most women in Colonial America received no formal education, many participated in businesses outside of the home. Marriage and motherhood were expected of every female in the eighteenth century.[44] Women in Colonial America were viewed as reproduction factories, not as free individuals. Furthermore, upon marriage a woman would lose her status under the law as a single woman, known as "coverture," which means the legal cover of her husband. This law dissolved married women's personal legal identity and rights of property and ownership; this meant that women could not pursue legal action but relied on their husbands to do so on their behalf. Since women could not legally own property, their material possessions technically belonged to their husbands. From modern perspectives, today's society would assume that women aspired to gain independence, but this situation was generally accepted in Colonial America as well as in England and was expected for women as they entered into marriage.[45] There were also women who opted to the legal status of *femme sole*, or *woman alone*, meaning a woman without a husband, especially one who is divorced. Few women chose this path and those who did were permitted "legally" to economically partake in the world outside of the traditional female gender roles; however, when he put a ring on it (marriage) she was relinquished of all she had earned when they married.[46] So basically, the woman became the property of the husband. Everything she earned was no longer her personal possession but the possession of her husband. Sounds like a form of slavery to me.

In 1757, John Brown published a book titled *An Estimate on the Manners and Principles of the Times*. He stated that sermon by religious philosophical and scientific arguments explained, rationalized, and legitimized that women needed supervision by men and that this was a natural occurrence.[47] Most research has been accepted as a fundamental and self-evident truth that eighteenth-century men's and women's lives were defined by starkly contrasting and increasingly rigid gender roles, most specifically exemplified by increasing confinement of women to a private, separate, domestic sphere.[48] Even though Colonial life created a divergence between genders, many American women abandoned the roles traditionally taught to them by their mothers and society. Soldiers, no matter the gender, are created out of citizen material, that which he or she brings a mental attitude of determination to govern by the desires of freedom. The brave women in this book assumed the role of a traditionally male soldier because they were disinclined to stand by and do nothing while the life they knew was in danger of being stripped away from a monarchy unwilling to provide freedom for its subjects.

There are several examples of warrior-like women. Women like the French peasant girl Joan of Arc, who later became a soldier (while dressed as a man) and led the French Army into victory over the English in the Siege of Orléans in 1429. Because this woman was a threat to endanger male dominance, she was captured by the Anglo-Burgundians and burned at the stake in 1431. Another great example is the Boudica (or Boudicca) Celtic Queen of the British Iceni Tribe. Roman historians Publius Cornelius Tacitus and Cassius Dio wrote that when her husband Prasutagas died without leaving a male heir, the Roman Empire confiscated the queen's land and property. They also publicly flogged Boudica and raped her two daughters. As vengeance for this violation, Boudica led an uprising against the Roman Empire around A.D. 60. She defeated the Ninth Legion and destroyed the Roman capital. However, in the end she was defeated by Roman General Gaius Suetonius Paulinus (A.D. 61).

When the call to take up arms came knocking at their door, these warrior-women of 1775 did not consider the consequences, the punishments if they were discovered, or fear of death, injury, and the possibility of sexual violence. However, the roles of these brave women who fought for liberty are not well known to the public through publications of historic literature relating to the Revolutionary War. Military historian John Keegan once stated warfare is the only one human activity from which women, with the most significant exceptions, have always and everywhere stood apart. Either Mr. Keegan had never heard the stories of female soldiers in the Revolutionary War, or he willingly chose to ignore them. While researching the Revolutionary War it is undetermined on how many women actually fought as men in battles. Diminishing these women's roles voids the general understanding of women during this era. The experience of women and men during the time the historian is researching. History of females should be placed back into the historical narrative, heroines should be recorded and not hidden from society like a Scarlet Letter. [49] According to historian Dr. Bettany Hughes, women only occupy around 0.5 percent of recorded history when they make up fifty percent of the population.[50] The profiles of women who bravely fought in battles against Great Britain gave their sweat, blood, and lives, all for the hope of freedom for those who wish to be free.

In 2016, the United States *Journal Slate Magazine* surveyed six hundred and fourteen books about history and discovered only seventy-five-point-eight percent of those books were written by men about war and U.S. presidents, and twenty-one percent of those books were biographies about men, which demonstrates there is a gap in history written about women. By focusing on one side of history, society's understanding will be incomplete and narrow. Michael Crichton once said that "the purpose of history is to explain the present to say why the world is the way it is."[51] The profanity of that statement is that Crichton says that the purpose of history is to tell us why the world is the way it is, then past, told preserved and retold, has a problem. If historians continue to write history the way it has been written, then history will remain to have only a one-sided narrative. A male narrative. Every time I pass a bookstore I stop and look in the history section, skimming the titles, the overwhelming majority of history books pertaining to war written about men. Women are excluded even though we are currently 51% (as of 2022) of the population in America.

As the thirteen United colonies struggled for their independence, it gave some women the opportunity to demonstrate their capacity to assume male responsibilities, such as taking over businesses, protecting the home front, and other masculine duties while their husbands were away fighting in the Continental Army. However, some women broke the rules of social convention by gathering intelligence for the Continental Army and became soldiers on the battlefield(s). Many women who lived alone left their children with family or friends to join the Continental Army for steady income; some joined for the opportunity to prove their worth. A private in the Continental Army earned $6.23 per month and pay would increase upon promotion of rank.[52] That is if they were paid. The beginning of the Continental Army enlistments were six months. On June 26, 1776, the Second Continental Congress offered a bounty of $10.00 for those who would enlist for three years, a bounty regarded by Army leaders as wholly insufficient.[53] Please note that throughout this book, I will describe battles' narratives. The descriptions are not a step-by-step account of the battles these brave women partook in. The sole purpose of this book is to provide an idea of what hardships they went through and to recognize it.

"I raise up my voice—not so I can shout, but so that those without a voice can be heard…we cannot succeed when half of us are held back."
- Malala Yousafzai, Nobel Peace Prize winner

ANNE BAILEY

Anne Bailey was born in 1742 in Liverpool, England; her maiden name was Anne Hennis. Anne came to America after she was orphaned in 1761; she came as an indentured servant.[54] According to a newspaper article dated 1934, her father served under the Duke of Marlborough and was wounded at the Battle of Blenheim (August 1704 War of the Spanish Succession). The Bell family (Joseph and Elizabeth) paid for her voyage. After all, there were few options an orphaned teenager would have in Liverpool. The speculation of her being an indentured servant can be plausible because it was costly to board a ship and cross the ocean to the New World. How else could an orphan afford a voyage? So, she boarded a ship (name unknown) with other destitute people with an estimated 300 poor folks in the bow of the ship practically starving, living in filth and disease, and a lot of those poor people didn't make it to America, but Anne was very young and strong. When the passengers docked, many poor individuals could not pay the captain for their voyage. Human cargo was profit, and if you couldn't pay for the journey you were to be sold. Captains did not care about separating moms from their children and husbands from wives. Besides, money was money to them. When Anne got off the ship, the Bell family waited for her. She was indentured to the Bell family for a total of four years. When her indentured servant contract ended, she married a Virginian settler named Richard Trotter and had one son, William. Richard taught Anne how to hunt, chop wood, track animals, and harvest corn. It was their little utopia, living independently with their son.

On April 30, 1774, a group of winter-grade white renegade trappers known as the Virginian Long Knives (a term used by the Iroquois meaning British colonists of VA), led by Daniel and Jacob Greathouse and 21 men, murdered a group of Iroquois and the entire family of the Mingo Chief Logan (part of Iroquoian), leader of one of the Six Nations of the Iroquois Confederacy. After Chief Logan's family and other tribal members were murdered, Chief Logan went on a warpath. Honestly, what would you do if somebody murdered your family and neighbors (you liked)? This savagery is known as the Yellow Creek Massacre. This incident contributed to the outbreak of Lord Dunmore's war, May through October 1774. It was said that Greathouse brothers took the scalps of their Indigenous foes and dangled them from his belt.[55] Because the tensions between American settlers and the Indigenous tribes had increased, in 1774 Virginia Governor John Murray and Lord Dunmore organized a border militia. Anne's husband enlisted in the Virginia Colonial Militia on October 10, 1774. Richard was KIA (Killed In Action) at the battle of Point Pleasant, known as the Battle of Kanawha, which the Continental Congress called the first battle of the American Revolution. Chief of the Shawnee tribe, Cornstalk, attacked the fort and was defeated by Colonel Andrew Lewis and 1,100 Virginia militiamen. After the defeat, Cornstalk signed a treaty with Lord Dunmore.

Anne grieved all winter long after she was told of her husband's death. She swore to avenge her husband's death and that the Shawnee and the British would pay. So, she left her seven-year-old son in the care of close friends. She then disguised herself as a man and became a scout, hunted, was a courier, spy, and soldier; she was known to carry a hatchet and a long rifle. She also hunted and killed as many of the "savages" as she could. The natives and settlers called Anne "Mad Anne" and the White Squaw of the Kanawha. We can only assume the natives and the colonists thought Anne as mad because of how she lived her life, which was very unconventional of a white female of that era. She lived in the wilderness under the stars and not conforming to traditional Colonial housewife values. The Indigenous tribes in the area thought Anne as being "charmed" or possessed by a demon. The definition of charmed to the Indigenous people is *"an individual who is not quite right in the head"* (in other words, a crazy person), and this probably saved her life in the wilderness. Indigenous people did not bother her because of this.

During the American Revolution, she aided the cause of the new nation by drumming up support for the Patriot militia and the Continental Army by encouraging men to volunteer. She rode from one recruiting station to another, later boasting, *"I always carried an ax and hauger, and I would chop as well as any man."* She also volunteered as a frontier messenger for the Colonial forces; she frequently traveled a 160-mile route between Fort Savannah (now Lewisburg) and Fort Randolph at Point Pleasant. In 1785 she married for a second time, to a John Bailey, who died in 1825. Her most famous exploit was in 1791, when Fort Lee (located present-day Charleston, West Virginia) was under siege by Shawnees. When the fort's gunpowder supply ran low, Ann in the dead of night got on the fastest horse the fort had and raced to Fort Savannah (100 miles away) and returned on the third day with the gunpowder, thereby saving the men in the Fort. She was 49 years old at the time. Lord Dunmore won this skirmish and the Shawnee never bothered the fort again. Evidence of this event appeared in print in 1860 by travel writer Anne Royall's *Sketches of History, Life, and Manners in the United States*. In her book, she stated that during the Revolutionary War, Bailey *"would shoulder her rifle, hang her shot-pouch over her shoulder, and lead a horse laden with ammunition to the Army, two hundred miles distant, when not a man could be found to undertake the perilous task."*[56] There is a family story passed down through the generations, of which many say is true but some say it is too wide to be:

On one occasion, when she was pursued by Indians, she came to an impenetrable thicket where she was obliged to dismount and leave him [her fine black horse, Liverpool] for their capture. She then crawled into a hollow sycamore log. The Indians came and rested on the log, but without suspecting her concealment within. After they had gone she followed their trail, and in the darkness of night recaptured the animal, and, when at a safe distance from being shot or taken gave a shout of defiance and bounded away.

Fort Lee, West Virginia

There's a famous poem about her by Charles Robb in 1861. Charles was a Civil War soldier and after the Battle of Phillippi (June 1861) the soldiers camped near Gauley Bridge and around the campfire, where he heard the story of Mad Anne being told from a West Virginia mountain man.

"Mad Anne" Bailey

"MAD" she was, this husky eccentric woman who lived to be eighty-two with a lust for revenge in her stout heart and donned a man's clothes to right her wrong in a man's way. For even in the lusty days of the late eighteenth century, when the mountains of Virginia were still frontier and harbored hostile Indians, no sane woman deserted her infant to live alone a man's life and start her own private collection of Indian scalps. The madness first descended upon Ann Bailey, then Anne Trotter, when her young husband fell victim to Indian cruelty at the battle of Point Pleasant. She was by 23 at the time, and only ten years behind her was the safe city life of Liverpool, England, where she was born. When the news reached her, she was like one possessed. She turned her baby boy over to a kindly neighbor, discarded her soft women's clothes for trousers and a hunting shirt, and shouldered a gun and with her horse, named Liverpool, turned her back up on her Staunton. Thereafter as "Mad Anne," she lived alone in a hut built with her own hands on the ridge of Covington Mountain in Allegheny County. From this vantage spot she watched the movements of the Indians in the surrounding countryside. Her most famous deed occurred at Fort Lee near Charleston, WV, in 1792, when Annie was 49 years old. Here, for safety during an Indian attack, she had gathered the settlers from the surrounding territory. The siege was a long one, and the powder supply had given out. Mad Anne volunteered aid. Mounting Liverpool, she rode out, in full view of the attacking Indians, then surrounding the horses into headlong speed. She flew past their lines, onto Fort Union, now Louisburg, where she secured powder and an extra horse. She returned the savior of the fort.

Mad Anne died on November 22, 1825, peacefully in her sleep surrounded by a few grandchildren (she had ten in total) by the fireplace in her cabin she made herself. Her remains were relocated from Ohio, where she died, to the Point Pleasant Battle Monument State Park (October 10, 1901), where the museum

Source: Monument State (West VA) Park at Point Pleasant

contains memorabilia of Anne including a design made from her hair (that's not creepy). As my grandmother would say, she was one tough cookie!

Historian Virgil A. Lewis, West Virginia's first state historian, wrote the following about Ann in 1910:

> *All that was earthly of Anne Bailey, the Pioneer heroine of the Great Kanawha Valley, that has not crumbled to dust, has been removed to Point Pleasant and re-interred in Tu-Endie-Wei Park. It is, therefore, now time to eliminate from the story of her wonderful career and life of adventure, as scout and messenger, everything of a mythical, legendary, fabulous and fanciful character, and to learn to know the real narrative—the truth—regarding that record female heroism which has no parallel in the annals of the Border Wars.*

Source: Point Pleasant, WV – Grave of Anne Bailey
Tombstone was unveiled in 2002

Source: Sketch, *"Anne Bailey, Frontier Scout,"* by Mary R. Furber
Morgan Reynolds Publishing, Inc., Greensboro, NC

The keeping of her grave is now in care of the Colonel Charles Lewis Chapter, Daughters of the American Revolution. Anne Bailey was herself a Daughter of the Revolution, a real one, who served her country faithfully and well when that struggle was in progress. Then this western border was the "Back Door of the Revolution," and the men and women who kept back from it the savage allies of Great Britain were the "Rear Guard of the Revolution." Anne Bailey was one of these, and schoolchildren should be able to tell the thousands who will henceforth visit her tomb the real story of her life.

"A strong woman stands up for herself.
A stronger woman stands up for everybody else."
- Eleanor Roosevelt

ANNA MARIA LANE

Anna Maria Lane was born around the 1730s and was the first documented female soldier in Virginia. On June 17, 1775, Mr. and Mrs. Lane enlisted for three years in the Continental Army in the 3rd New Hampshire Regiment.[57] On July 22, 1775, the regiment became an element of the Main Continental Army, commanded by Colonel James Reed. Anna was both a camp follower and disguised herself as a male soldier.[58] Historian Harry M. Ward writes that Mrs. Lane enlisted, along with her husband, in the Continental Army disguised as a man. She enlisted under the name of John Lane Jr., age forty-two (Anna and John only had a daughter).[59] Some historians state that Anna Maria never dressed as a man on the battlefield; however, enlisting as John Lane Jr. is evidence that she did dress as a man to disguise herself as a man. Anna cut off her long, beautiful hair, possibly bandaged her breasts, and tailored her husband's clothes to fit her so she could appear as a man. Her courageous behavior is the definition of bravery. Anna made a courageous choice in leaving her young daughter behind to fight for freedom.

Source: Marker honoring Anna, Richmond, VA, erected 1997

This Patriot had virtually been forgotten until the discovery of the Virginia Pension records in 1928 by the editor of the *Richmond Magazine*, John Archer Carter. He also presented an article to the *Daughters of the American Revolution Magazine* in 1928, entitled "A Virginian Heroine." If it were not for Mr. Archer discovering Anna's pension requests in the Virginia Archives, she might have forever been lost. Below is Ann's enlistment record. This proves without a reasonable doubt that she did dress as a man.

Anna Maria and her husband fought in three battles side by side and were exposed to combat, long marches, extreme exhaustion, unwholesome food, and fear of ambushes

L | Reed's Regiment. | **N. H.**

John Lane, Jr.

Appears with the rank of .... on a

List *

of Cap¹ Hezekiah Hutchins' Comp⁴ June 9, 1775,
(**Revolutionary War.**)

dated .... June 17, 1775.

age 42

occupation .... Cordwainer

place of abode .... Chester

County .... Rockingham

Remarks:

* From copy (verified in the R. & P. Office in Nov., 1895,) of an
original record borrowed from the State of New Hampshire.—
R. & P. 411,721.

(646m)   Copyist.

Source: U.S. Compiled Revolutionary War Military Service Records, 1775-1783
(database online), New Hampshire: Reed's Regiment

from the British or Indigenous tribes. Anna marched to wherever her company was dispatched; be it New York, New Jersey, Pennsylvania, or back to her native colony, she marched. Anna's name is amongst America's immortal Patriots of the Revolutionary War. However, outside of her home state she is hardly known to the rest of the world. The first battle fought together was at the Battle of White Plains, NY, on October 28, 1776 (which was of the larger invasion of New York City).

The battle involved General George Washington, along with 3,100 troops, militias, and Indigenous allies. The British commander was General William Howe, with 7,500 soldiers, the Iroquois, and German Hessian mercenaries. Initially, General Howe attempted to land his ships at Throggs Neck. However, he faced resistance and turned to Apelles' Point. Howe was at a disadvantage. He used unreliable maps that made his troops move slowly because they were in unfamiliar territory.

Two weeks before the battle of White Plains occurred, General Washington issued General orders. They read as follows:

> *How much better it would be to die honorably, fighting in the field than to run home covered with shame and disgrace, even if the cruelty of the enemy should allow you to return a brave and gallant behavior for a few days and patience under some little hardship may save our country and enable us to go into winter quarters with safety and honor.*

General Washington and Howe understood that whoever controlled New York would control the Hudson River. Washington stationed most of his troops in White Plains, which had proved incompatible for military maneuvering, so he chose that location for the battle. The Continental Army dug two long entrenchments parallel, stretching across the line of the hills above White Plains from the top of Purdy Hill at a point immediately east of the Bronx River and eastward over Rocky Heights to Merritt Hill, on the east side of Silver Lake. An estimated 600 troops were on Chatterton Hill. British forces stormed the hill in three separate divisions and were forced back twice. The third time the British General called in the Hessian mercenaries, who moved strategically through the

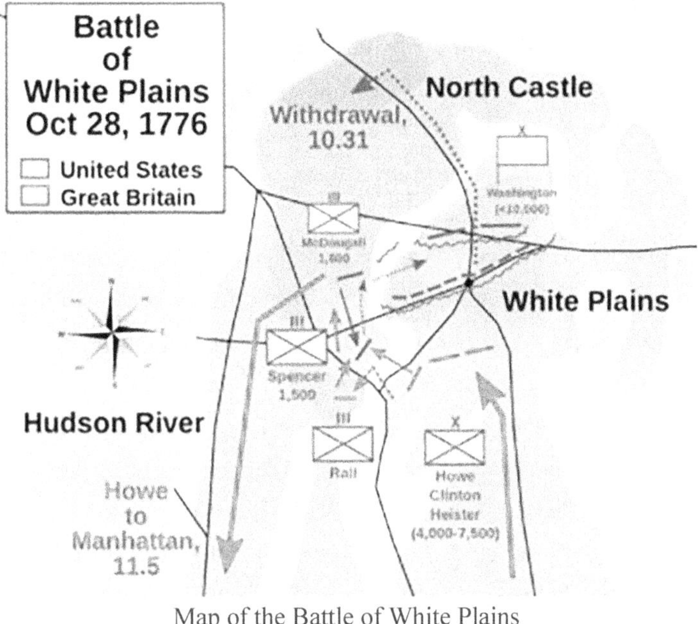

Map of the Battle of White Plains

woods toward the right flank of the Continental Army in a surprise attack; the American army's defensive positions were overrun. Washington ordered a withdrawal with the 1st Delaware Regiment guarding the rear. This resulted in the British occupying the hill. On October 30 additional Hessian and Waldeck troops arrived. Howe intended to attack the following day. However, a heavy rain fell the whole next day, and when Howe was finally prepared to act he awoke to find Washington under cover of darkness. General Washington escaped and moved his troops to Manhattan. Once again, General Howe missed the opportunity to capture Washington and his troops. This victory allowed the British to gain control over the mouth of the Hudson River.[60] The British only suffered 233 casualties and Washington suffered an estimated 270 casualties.

The second battle was at the Battle of Princeton, which took place on January 3, 1777, and lasted nine days. General Charles Cornwallis' British commander had 1,200 soldiers with only 270 casualties. The American commander was General Washington, with an estimated 4,500 troops with militia being commanded under Brigadier General John Cadwalader. Washington had thirty-five artillery pieces and only had seventy-five casualties. Washington had another unusual battalion comprised of ethnic German colonials from Maryland and Pennsylvania, known as the German battalion, authorized by the Continental Congress in 1776 to be an extra Continental regiment. Nicholas Haussegger was the commander of the German battalion.[61] Washington's army, using a flank maneuver during the night, moved to Princeton, NJ, behind Cornwallis' army. Anna (John Lane Jr.) and her husband were involved in a tense fight involving bayonets designed to destroy the enemy in hand-to-hand combat and considered an offensive weapon. The purpose of a bayonet fighter is to attack swiftly and relentlessly assault until the enemy is destroyed.[62] General Washington chased the British Army off the battlefield and into Nassau Hall in Princeton, New Jersey. The Continental Army started firing their cannons at Nassau Hall, resulting in the British surrendering. Washington demonstrated his ability to unify soldiers from different colonies into an effective national force skilled of defeating the British Army in the field. This victory bolstered the morale throughout the Continental Army and provided confidence amongst the soldiers and militia. The American victory threatened the Crown's supply lines following this battle, and British forces pulled back to a more defensive position near the Hudson River, freeing much of New Jersey from British control. Fun fact: Another woman was also involved in his battle, Mary Ludwig Hays—you will learn about her in chapter three.

The final battle was the Battle of Germantown, which took place in Germantown, Pennsylvania, on October 4, 1777; the battle only lasted five hours.[63] The second Canadian Regiment (nicknamed Congress' Own) was also under General Washington. Washington launched a surprise attack. Washington's tactical plan was to hit Howe simultaneously with four columns converging from different directions.[64] In contrast, General John Sullivan's center-right column, General Nathanael Greene's center-left column, and Major General William Alexander, also known as Lord Stirling's reserve, were American Continentals.[65] Heavy fog confused both sides. An estimated one hundred or so British soldiers under the command of Colonel Musgrave took a fortified position in Chief Justice Benjamin Chew's stone mansion. The Americans launched numerous assaults resulting in heavy casualties. Bloody hand-to-hand fighting took place inside and outside the house before the Patriots were forced to retreat. This attack failed with severe losses. According to William Broaddus Cridlin's 1923 newspaper article,

"State Pensioned Brave Girl Who Fought as Man Until Severely Wounded at Germantown Battle," while charging the British ranks with her company in an effort to throw the enemy back, Anna was severely injured in the leg. [66]

Her comrades snatched her torn body from the ground and carried her to the medical tent. That was when her gender was discovered. Not one of her comrades knew that he was a she, except Mr. Jones. There are no known records of Anna Maria being court-martialed for impersonating a male soldier or even placed back in with the camp followers. The Continental Army threw down their arms and retreated in the thick fog, which granted the British a victory. The British victory in this battle ensured that Philadelphia, the capital of the self-proclaimed United States of America, would remain in the British hands throughout the winter of 1777 through 1778. [67]

On September 14, 1777, General Washington wrote a letter to Major General Israel Putnam. It stated:

> *The experience of the battle of Germantown has served to convince our people, that when they make an attack, they can confuse and Rout even the Flower of the British Army, with the greatest ease, and they are not that invincible Body of Men which many suppose them to be.* [68]

Superstitious Continental soldiers and militia believed that they were defeated because of bad luck, not poor tactics. At this point in the American Revolutionary War, the Continental Army took the offensive and attacked the British.

After Anna's husband was captured in the Siege of Savannah, GA, on December 29, 1778 (first Battle of Savannah), and later released, they enlisted in the Virginia Public Guard at Richmond. It is believed that many Revolutionary War combat veterans were worn out from the war; some without property or money suffered from Post-Traumatic Stress Disorder (undiagnosed at the time). These tired veterans needed to have a purpose. Many who faithfully served their country during the American Revolution continued their enlistment as State Public Guards. John and Anna were stationed at Point of Fork, Columbia, Virginia, on the James River near Charlottesville. The installation was responsible for supplying the state militias with services, weapons, and clothing. Anna and her daughter were household workers. They received a small wage.[69]

Even though Anna Maria Lane was a female and females were not permitted to be soldiers, the Virginia State Guard honored her as a veteran of the Revolutionary War and allowed her to join as a soldier. Anna served as a nurse until 1807. She tended to the guardsmen as an assistant to the city's physician. Both John and Anna Maria were discharged from the Virginia State Guard in 1808, one because they were in their eighties and two because their combat wounds practically infirmed them.[70]

While going through the Virginia Archives pertaining to the pension requests, a letter was discovered, written by Governor William Campbell to the speaker of the Virginia House of Delegates, in 1808, requesting a pension for Anna. It states the following:

> *In awarding a military pension to Anna Maria Lane, the Virginia Assembly noted that she was "very infirm, having been disabled by a severe wound, which she received while fighting as a common soldier ... from which she never recovered." And, further: "In the Revolutionary War, in the garb, and with the courage of a soldier, [she] performed extraordinary military services at the Battle of Germantown." For her "extraordinary military services" she was awarded an immediate grant. And then, for the remainder of her life, she collected a quarterly pension payment of $25 (her husband, meanwhile, collected payments of $10 every quarter).*[71]

In 1808, Mr. and Mrs. Lane both received pensions. Mr. Lane received the typical forty dollars a year, dispersed quarterly. Anna received one hundred dollars a year, because she "in the Revolutionary War, in the garb, and with the courage of a soldier, performed extraordinary military services, and received a severe wound at the battle of Germantown." Her pension was two and a half times the sum of her male counterparts.[72] One may never know what part Anna Maria Lane actually played, but it is evident she participated as a soldier. Anna Maria Lane died in Virginia in 1810.[73] There are several blogs and state historical societies dedicated

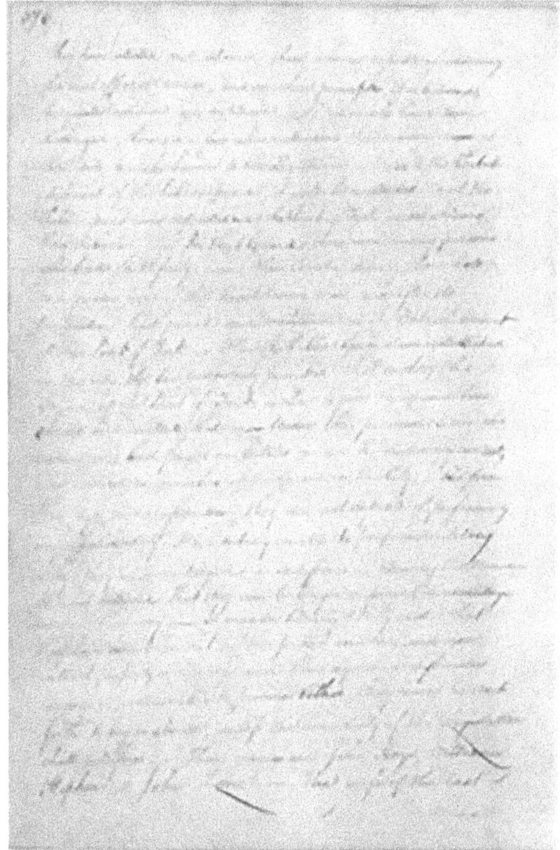

Source: William Cabell's letter to the speaker of the Virginia Assembly, posted by the Library of Virginia

to Anna Maria Lane, and a few history books such as *Anna Maria Lane: An Uncommon Soldier of the American Revolution,* by Gioia Treadway, and *Women and the Revolutionary War,* by Kaia K. Danyluk, mention her. [74]

Anna Maria Lane faced the possibility of being killed in battle, just like all soldiers in the Continental Army, and she faced the daily hardships of war, dealt with hunger, endured extreme weather, the trauma of seeing dead bodies, and the act of stepping into a soldier's role, which was pure heroism. Unfortunately, there are no written records or journals stating exactly what Anna Maria Lane did on the battlefield other than what the pension records stated. Anna was a spectacular hero; her patriotic service and sacrifices for her country should never be forgotten.

CHAP. XCVII.

An Act placing on the list of Pensioners certain Persons therein named.

[Passed February 6, 1808.]

1 BE it enacted by the General Assembly, That John Hays and Nancy his wife, William Hipkins and Judith his wife, Robert Broadus, Sarah Perry, widow of Hildebert Perry, Kitty Barlow, widow of John Barlow, deceased, John Lane and Anna Maria his wife, shall be, and are hereby placed on the list of pensioners; and the eight of them first named, shall be entitled to receive annually from the public treasury, the sum of forty dollars each; and the said Anna Maria, who in the revolutionary war, in the garb, and with the courage of a soldier, performed extraordinary military services, and received a severe wound, at the battle of German-Town, shall in consideration thereof, be entitled to receive one hundred dollars per annum, from the public treasury. Each of the pensioners herein named shall also be authorised to receive the sum of forty dollars for their immediate relief, and the auditor of public accounts is required to issue his warrants therefor, payable out of any money in the treasury.

2. This act shall be in force from the passing thereof.

Certain persons placed on pension list.

Commencement

Anna Maria Lane's Pension (An Incomplete Notation)

Anna Maria Lane was illiterate and signed for her pension by marking the receipt with an X.

Source: Letter, William H. Cabell to Speaker of the House of Delegates. January 28, 1808. Manuscript. RG 3, Governor's Office, Executive Letter Books, William H. Cabell, July 8, 1807 – March 9, 1808. The Library of Virginia, Richmond, Virginia

In the book *Revolutionary Mothers* by Carol Berkin, published in 2005, [75] the author discusses that thousands of women and children followed the Continental Army as camp followers to perform domestic duties for the soldiers. The author briefly speaks about women crossing gender lines. Two sentences, to be exact. She mentions Anna Marie Lane who, when her husband enlisted in the Continental Army, donned men's clothing and enlisted with him; nothing more was added. The author also mentions that Ann Bailey, who enlisted under Samuel Gray, was discharged and in jail for two weeks after her sex was discovered. No additional information was provided. As you can see from reading about Anna Maria Lane, more than two sentences must be contributed to her. This woman was indeed an extraordinary individual. I would also like to note that I currently live in Virginia and my daughters also went to school (K-12) here. And I had never heard of Anna Maria Lane until I started conducting my research on female soldiers of the Revolutionary War. Virginia is doing a disservice to this hero by not teaching school-aged children and National Guard members about the first recorded female soldier of Virginia. Shame on you, Virginia!

"Being brave meant that though you might be frightened,
you would face the greatest danger if you knew it was the right thing to do."
– Anne Holm (Danish journalist)

MARGARET CATHERIN MOORE BARRY

Margaret Catherine Moore Barry (a.k.a. Kate Moore Barry) was born on November 29, 1752, in Antrim, Ireland.[76] Many falsely claim that she was born in South Carolina. In 1763 she and her family immigrated to America. Later that year her father, Charles Moore Sr. (mother was Mary), received a land grant in South Carolina and named their new land the Walnut Grove Plantation, located in Spartanburg County. In 1767, at fifteen she married Andrew Barry and lived on her parents' plantation. Her husband became a captain in the militia under Major Henry White and Colonel John Thomas Jr. Margaret had five sons and six daughters. Noted on the Sons of the American Revolutionary War supplemental application, Margaret was ever on the watch for evidence of danger or trouble in her neighborhood. She would warn the women and children to flee to Fort Nicholas or Fort Prince for safety since many families in the region had been massacred by Indigenous tribes. With the aid of the faithful colored man, Margaret kept her friends fully informed and the local Patriot militias were never taken by surprise. Now this was all around where she lived. On one occasion, Margaret overheard Tories crossing the Tyger River at her father's house, so she tied her baby to the bedpost and rode as fast as possible to get help. She was then captured by the local Tories; Margaret was brave and refused to give information about the whereabouts of her husband's company, so the Tories tied her up and struck her three times with a lash.

Margaret was involved in the Battle of Cowpens (January 1781). On the Patriot side was Brigadier General Daniel Morgan. General Nathanael Greene sent Morgan with 600 Continentals plus Thomas Sumter's militia to fight in the battle.[77] The British was led by Lieutenant Colonel Sir Banastre Tarleton. Tarleton was ordered by General Cornwallis to turn his attention to Morgan. The British saw Morgan as a threat to their left flank. Morgan knew Tarleton continuously illustrated a will to quickly close with and destroy his enemy through audacity, tempo, and often reckless fighting and so he adapted to Tarleton's tactics.[78] Morgan laid out a plan intended to use the Redcoats' (British) confidence against them. In total, Tarleton commanded approximately 1,150 soldiers.[79] The Continental Army was comprised of 300 infantries from two states, approximately 550 total militia from surrounding states. In total, the Continental Army strength was approximately

800 to 1,100 Continental and militia forces. Morgan began pulling his troops back, staying miles ahead of the British to spread his men out to ensure they could find forage. Moran made the call for all available militia to join him and requested a scout to go seek more soldiers. Who do you think that might have been? You are correct, it was Margaret, who was part of General Morgan's third South Carolina Rangers. She was commissioned as a scout because she was familiar with the wilderness and Indigenous trails. Scouts operated covertly to obtain, distribute, and share vital intelligence on enemy forces. Margaret accepted her orders from General Morgan and rode out to give the call to arms and assembled Patriots and hurried them back to fight in the battle of Cowpens.[80]

Margaret's husband was Captain of the Rangers; perhaps that was how she was able to join. Mr. Berry's Rangers fought at Cedar Springs and Musgrove's Mill (1780) battles, both won by the Patriots. The assumption is that Margaret also participated in these battles, to what extent it is unclear. In a short time, General Morgan found himself with sufficient forces added to his line army of four hundred regulators to give battle. Margaret also gathered South Carolina Rangers by crossing rivers, evading Tories, and encountered other dangers. By the time the Continental Army and the Patriot militia allowed the British Army to catch up with them at Cowpens, General Morgan's army was one thousand six hundred troops strong. Morgan delayed action to get his command up to full strength. Morgan arrived at the Broad River and waited for the pursuing Redcoats.[81] It was about to go down!

Rangers, scouts (including Margaret), and the newly gathered militiamen kept a close eye on Tarleton; they also cut down trees to slow down the Redcoats' artillery and wagons and set fires near the roads, all in an attempt to delay the British as much as possible. Morgan arranged his men in three battle lines. The first were the sharpshooters, who were one hundred and fifty yards in front of the militia line. Second, the militia, which consisted of surrounding states. The third was Commander Howard's Continentals Army, and finally William Washington's Dragoons (cavalry).[82]

Margaret Catherin Moore Barry succeeded in presenting Morgan's little army with sufficient forces to bring off the best fight of the Revolution at that time, when all seemed lost to the Patriotic cause, and so followed Carolina's

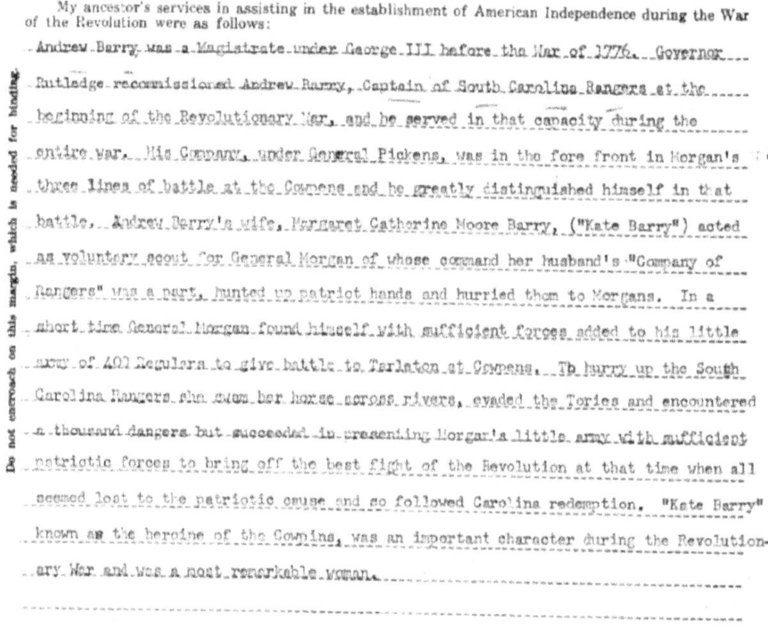

Original data: Sons of the American Revolution Membership Applications, 1889-1970. Louisville, Kentucky: National Society of the Sons of the American Revolution. Microfilm, 508 rolls.

Source: Sons of the American Revolution Membership Applications, 1889-1970. Louisville, Kentucky;

National Society of the Sons of the American Revolution. Microfilm, 508 roll.

redemption. Margaret, known as the heroine of the Cowpens, was an important character during the Revolutionary War. [83] Margaret's knowledge of the terrain made her an invaluable soldier. In fact, her services proved to make a difference in the outcome of the Revolutionary War. In the end, the British had an estimated one hundred and ten casualties, over two hundred wounded, and five hundred captured by the Patriots. The Continentals had an estimated twelve casualties, with sixty wounded. This engagement further weakened British attempts to advance in their Southern Campaign.[84]

Source: Kate Barry Marker
South Carolina,
in Spartanburg County

Margaret Berry is a celebrated hero in South Carolina. After reviewing countless newspaper articles published in South Carolina that recount her heroic deeds in the Revolutionary War, I noticed those newspapers were the only ones referring to her brave accounts. The rest of society is absent from her patriotic adventures in the Revolutionary War. On South Carolina's website, I ventured to the National Park Service national battlefield of Cowpens. The National Park puts on a play titled "A Scary Day for Kate Berry." However, the website section titled "Voices of the Revolution during the 230th-Anniversary Event," the National Park noted Kate Berry has a husband and brother who both fought in the battle with the Cowpens; however, it did not mention anything about her recruiting the militia needed for this battle to be successful. And I love how they always refer to her as Kate Berry. That was a nickname; her legal name is Margaret. Using a nickname confuses readers and future historians.

Margaret Catherine Moore Barry continues to be recognized in South Carolina, especially since her house was deemed a historical landmark. However, what about the rest of the country? Now, you have learned about the hero of Cowpens, Margaret died a hero on September 29, 1823. She was buried next to her husband in his family cemetery near Moore, South Carolina.[85] The strangest thing, really—today is September 29th, 2022, and I am writing about Margaret. Coincidence?

"Heroes get remembered, but legends never die."
—Babe Ruth

PRUDENCE CUMMINGS WRIGHT

Mrs. Prudence Cummings Wright was born November 26, 1740, in Dunstable, Massachusetts. She grew up in a divided home. Some of her family members were very loyal to the king, while others were greatly displeased with how the king was treating his people. She was the disappointed one. In 1761, Prudence (age 21) married David Wright, a Whig and an avid supporter of independence. They had seven children and lived only twenty miles northwest of Concord, Massachusetts. While researching women soldiers of the American Revolutionary War, I came across Prudence Cummings Wright's name in a book titled *An Encyclopedia of American Women at War [2 volumes]: From the Home Front to the Battlefields*. However, only a short blurb about the Minutewomen was mentioned. Fascinated, I discovered more evidence on the Massachusetts historical society. Another book Mrs. Cummings Wright was mentioned in was published by Susan Casey, titled *Women Heroes of the American Revolution: Twenty Stories of Espionage, Sabotage, Defiance, and Rescue*. This book recited what the historical society published, which was only a few sentences. How were the militiawomen created, and who was the leader? So many questions to be answered, and two sentences in both references noted above did not provide the answers. So below is what I discovered about Prudence.

Prudence grew concerned about her widowed mother, who lived in Hollis, MA, and decided to go visit her. While visiting, she overheard men and her brother Thomas (who was a Tory, another brother was also a Tory) speaking in a tavern that spies might pass by these parts from Canada down to Boston with intelligence useful to the British troops. Mrs. Wright quickly went back to Pepperell, telling all the townspeople of the conversation she overheard. On April 18, 1775, British Commander-in-Chief of North America Thomas Gage marched his troops to Concorde, Massachusetts, to seize a cachet of arms (it was rumored that the colonials had this) and capture the rebel leaders Samuel Adams and John Hancock (they escaped). Paul Revere got wind of this plan and road out to warn the Colonialists. On April 19, 1775, the Minutemen in Groton, Hollis, and Pepperell, MA, marched to the battle in Lexington and Concord, leaving their mothers, sisters, and wives vulnerable. This would be the first battle of the American Revolutionary War. When the Redcoats were face to face with hundreds of militiamen, they were shocked that there would be a standoff, which resulted in everyone's tensions being high. No one on either side wanted to give the command to fire the first shot. However, someone did fire the first shot. Neither side admits it fired the first shot (same thing happened in the Civil War). Colonial militia fled to Concord, and the British were unable to locate the hidden weapons. There was a total of three thousand, nine hundred and sixty Minutemen, and fifteen hundred British troops. The Americans only suffered ninety-three casualties; however, the British suffered three hundred.

With all able-bodied men fighting in the battle of Lexington and Concord, Mrs. Prudence Cummings Wright took it upon herself to defend her town by creating Minutewomen. This militia consisted of thirty to forty women from surrounding counties (Groton and Hollis) who took their husbands' and brothers' clothing, disguising themselves as men and armed with muskets and pitchforks. The lieutenant was a woman named Sarah Shattuck (1738-1798), wife of Captain Job Shattuck, mother of nine children. This is the extent of my research; I cannot locate anything further on her. Unfortunately, every time I pick up a book to read about the battle of Lexington and Concord, it never mentions the Minutewomen who were also involved. Why is that? Did historians not know this historical fact? Or was this gender bias? So many questions once again with no answers.

The Minutewomen patrolled the forests and Jewett's Bridge[86] over the Nashua River to prevent British troops from passing through their town. The Minutewomen assembled a few days after the battles of Lexington and Concord began; they patrolled the bridge night and day, until they received intelligence that British forces were expected travel their way. Then one night, while expecting an army of British soldiers, two horsemen approached from the north. One was her brother Thomas and the other Captain Leonard Whiting, a known Tory (loyal to the British Crown). Captain Prudence ordered a halt. Prudence's brother, hearing her voice, said, *"Not one further step I ride!* He cried, *" 'Tis my sister Prue! Alas, she would never let me pass, she would wade through blood for the rebel cause. Save when her dead body fell!"* He turned back from Pepperell.

Thomas rode off, leaving Captain Whiting. He was easily captured by the Minutewomen, who intercepted British dispatches hidden in the captain's boot, which were addressed to the British General Thomas Gage of Boston. After taking the British Captain prisoner, the Minutewomen marched their prisoner through the neighborhoods to the middle of the town, detained, and guarded the prisoner until morning, then they handed Captain Whiting over to Major General Oliver Prescott of the Massachusetts militia. The Minutewomen disbanded after the delivery of the prisoner. The town of Pepperell was unable to pay the women for their bravery until a town meeting was called on March 19, 1777. Then Pepperell voted to pay Leonard Whiting's Guard[87] seven pounds, seventeen shillings and six pence. A sign by Jewett's Bridge states the following:

> *Near this spot a party of Patriotic women, under the leadership of Mrs. David Wright, of Pepperell, in April 1775, captured Leonard Whiting, a Tory who was carrying treasonable dispatches to the enemy at Boston. He was taken prisoner to Groton, and the dispatches were sent to the Committee of Safety at Cambridge.*[88]

When the time came, Prudence Cummings Wright and her Minutewomen prepared to defend their townspeople against the British Army and treasonous

Source: March 19, 1777, Town of Pepperell written record.
The guard was called "Leonard Whiting's Guard,"
after the British officer they captured.

colonists. These brave women did not hesitate. Their heroic actions demonstrated that their only concern was stopping the enemy. The Leonard Whiting's Guard only cared about the cause. These women's heroism matched the men who fought in the Revolutionary War.

David Wright returned home after the war; they lived a long life together and had a total of eleven children. Prudence died in 1823, her husband in 1819.

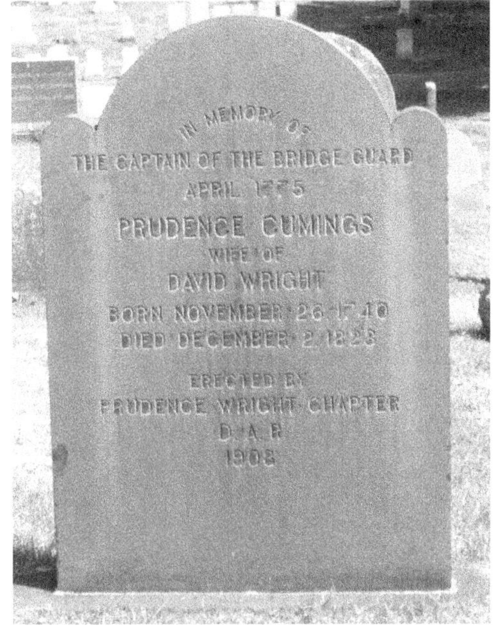

Source: Prudence's grave
Her epitaph reads: *In Memory of the Captain of the Bridge Guard.*

Source: grave of Sarah Shattuck

"Bravery is the capacity to perform properly even when scared half to death."
—Omar N. Bradley (Former General of the U.S. Army)

SALLY ST. CLAIR

Not much is known about Sally's personal life. In *True Stories of the Days of Washington*, first published in 1861, the anonymous author states that Sally was a beautiful dark-eyed Creole woman of color (African and French descent).[89] It is not known when she was born or who her parents were. What historians do know is that she enlisted in the Continental Army with her sweetheart, William Jasper, into the South Carolina 2nd South Carolina Regiment under the command of Lieutenant Colonel Francis Marion, known as The Swamp Fox (French and Indian War vet). She followed her lover not as a camp follower but as a soldier. While going through the regiment's muster rolls, I came across the name Private James St. Clair.[90] I am no rocket scientist nor have I ever claimed I was one. However, I am 99.9% sure that this is Sally St. Clair since she was disguised as a young man. In the many books and websites referring to William Jasper, he is referred to as Sergeant. Perhaps that is the rank he was discharged with, which is highly possible. However, according to the U.S. Revolutionary War payrolls, he is noted as Quartermaster. Jasper and Sally's regiment encompassed hit-and-run guerilla-type tactics against the British Army and Loyalist militias. Marion's irregular militiamen were known to be ruthless because they terrorized Loyalists. Marion's militia served without pay and supplied their own food, horses, and weapons.[91] Jasper and Sally's regiment was rarely committed to frontal warfare but constantly targeted larger bodies of Loyalists or British regulars with quick surprise attacks and equally sudden withdrawal from the field. Sort of like what Mel Gibson did in the movie *The Patriot* when the British captured his son and was escorting him to be executed as a spy. The actor hacked up the enemy before they could hang him. Sally's regiment also fought freed slaves that worked for and fought alongside the British.

In *True Stories of the Days of Washington*, the author preceded to romanticize Sally and Jasper's relationship, stating that *"separation from Jasper to her warm impulsive nature was almost maddening."* There's absolutely no evidence that Sally or Jasper said this. It was added to glamorize the story. The unknown author also stated that Sally attracted no particular attention; her disguise was so complete and none were more eager for the battle, so indifferent to fatigue as the smooth-faced boy. Side by side Sally and Jasper fought together in battles.

Jasper and Sally's regiment engaged in the following *"recorded"* battles: Charleston 1775 -1776 and Charleston 1780. Marion was tasked by General Gates to roam the Santee River, burning British and Tory boats to isolate Camden from Charleston, South Carolina. There were several skirmishes that Marion's militia took part in; they were Tearcoat Swamp on October 25, 1780; Battle of Black Mingo, Georgetown (four attacks), between October 1780 and May 1781; Fort Watson on April 23, 1781; Fort Motte on May 12, 1781; Quinby Bridge on July 17, 1781; Parker's Ferry on August 13, 1781; Eutaw Springs on September 8, 1781; Wadboo Plantation on August 29, 1782; and the Siege of Savanna 1779. On August 29, 1782, a British foraging party made up of white and black troops and commanded by Major Thomas Fraser attacked Brigadier General Francis Marion and his militiamen at Wadboo Swamp, where they had camped the night before. Since Lord Cornwallis' surrender at Yorktown three months prior (October 1781), many major battles had ceased. However, the British was still fighting to hold Charleston, which was under the command of British General Alexander. Regardless of Lord Cornwallis' surrender, Loyalist raiders were still committed to harassing Patriots and vice versa. It could be possible that those further south did not get word of Cornwallis' surrender. However, Yorktown and Charlotte, North Carolina, are only 438 miles apart. Hmm, it seems that many British troops and Loyalist militias did not want to go out without a fight. Therefore, the war was not winding down in the South.

In *Tales of Marion's Men* by Edward Willett, published in 1866, he states on the night before her final battle, she was noticed bending over Jasper's couch, like a good and gentle spirit, as if listening to his dreams.[92] On August 29, 1782, in the dead of night the camp was under a surprise attack by a British foraging party, made up of white and black troops and commanded by Major Thomas Fraser.[93] The two lovers sprang into action and once again found themselves side by side in the thickest of the fight. Marion had 299 men and one woman on his side and Fraser had 180 troops on his. The 2nd South Carolina Regiment suddenly found themselves out of the swamp and into the Wadboo plantation. Marion divided his forces, positioning themselves near and about the plantation's slave cabins and the main house. Marion's cavalry horses were six miles away, so they were useless. He devised a plan that *"drew up in an avenue of trees before the house a part of my Left Advanced a few paces under cover of three small houses."* With the surrounding lands of the Wadboo plantation otherwise cleared of trees, any advance by Fraser would be out in open fields. In *A Sketch of the Lie of Brigadier General Francis Marion*, author and firsthand eyewitness William Dobein James writes, "[Marion] occupied the mansion and his men the outhouses, on the west toward the bridge; on the back of the outhouses to the east, and directly in front of the dwelling, there stretched toward the road an extensive avenue of old cedar trees, 30 the trimming of which had been neglected for some years; and their long boughs now descended nearly to the ground. Gen. Marion heard of the approach of Major Fraser with the British cavalry, toward the Santee, in his rear. On this side, there was nothing but a mile-long open field."[94] While instituting a line within these trees, Marion sent forth Captain Gavin Witherspoon and a handful of officers who retained their horses to monitor the field for Fraser's approach. Within minutes, more than one hundred mounted Royalist Black Dragoons (part of the Black Carolina Corps) and a few Loyalist cavalry charged down Witherspoon's detachment. The British fell back, luring them closer to Marion. The bulk of the American militia stayed hidden behind cedar trees, waiting to ambush the British. Captain William Dobein James states, "Witherspoon had advanced little into the woods beyond the old field when the reconnoitering party were met by Major Fraser at the head of his cavalry corps and were immediately charged. A long chase commenced, which was soon observed by Marion, and he drew up his men under the thick boughs of the cedar trees. As the chase advanced toward him, it became more and more interesting. When in full view, either Witherspoon's horse had failed him, or he fell purposely in the rear to bring up his party, and a British dragoon was detached to cut him down. He advanced until nearly within his sword's length and was rising in his stirrups to make sure of his blow, but Witherspoon had eyed him well, and at the instant, Parthian like [rearward], he fired the contents of his gun into his breast. The good omen excited much animation."[95]

Fraser's dragoons came up to the avenue; within thirty yards, Marion's men rapidly fired into them from their hidden positions. In the heat of battle a British soldier was going to impale Jasper with his sword. Sally being right by his side stepped in front of Jasper and the sword impaled her heart instead. She fell dead at his feet. I have read some articles saying that it was a musket that was shot at Jasper instead of a sword. However, firsthand accounts in the two books I noted above state it was a sword. Jasper continued fighting or else he too would lay dead on the ground.

The Swamp Fox would write, "The fire was so well directed…that the Enemy immediately broke and retreated in confusion, leaving a Capt'n Robert Gillis and three men and five horses killed." Fraser regrouped his forces in an open field to the north of the house and other buildings, making sure he was out of musket range for either party. For one hour both sides did not budge an inch. Both expected calvary charges from one another. There were an estimated twenty casualties—three from the American militia and seventeen for the British. Oh, and one British solder captured. This battle is marked in history as inconclusive.

After the victory Jasper searched for his lover's body. And once found, her true name was spoken from his lips and her sex was revealed. Eyewitnesses stated that everyone in the regiment was shocked and came to tears when they discovered that James St. Clair was actually a female soldier who fought gallantly by their side all this time. Sally St. Clair was laid to rest in her grave, in a green shady nook near the Santee River, immediately after battle. The location of her grave is described as that it looked as if it had been stolen out of paradise.

IN THE MIDST OF THE BATTLE, WITH HER LOVER
BY HER SIDE, THE HEROIC MAIDEN DIES.

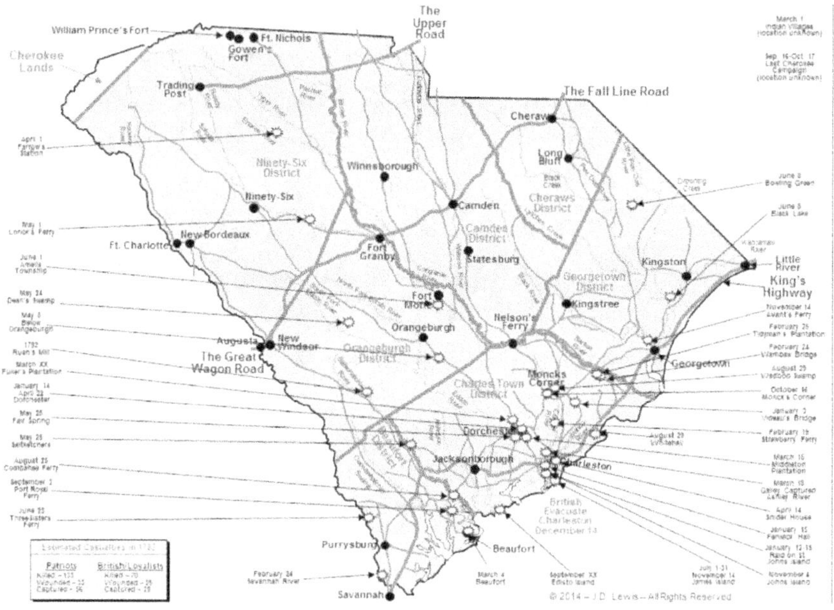

Source: J. D. Lewis, 2014 Map of battles that took place in SC in 1782

In *Revolutionary Mothers: Women in the Struggle for America's Independence,* Carol Berkin claims that Sally died during the Siege of Savannah in 1779 (2nd battle of Savannah).[96] The first battle of Savannah took place a year prior, on December 29th, 1778, which is also known as the Battle of Brewton Hill. In *True Stories of the Days of Washington,* published in 1872, the author states that Sally died in 1782. Which is it? Was it 1779 or 1782? The answer is she died in 1782 and we have evidence of that in poet George Pope Morris' poem, which states that Sally was buried near the Santee River, which is located in South Carolina and is 143 miles long. Savannah, GA, is roughly three hours away from the Santee River, and since she was buried immediately after the battle there is no way that the 2nd South Carolina regiment traveled 150 miles to bury Sally. The battle of Wadboo, August 29, 1782, is close to Santee River.

Poet George Pope Morris wrote a poem about Sally, which proves that she was *not* killed in the Siege of Savannah in 1779. One can only imagine the grief Jasper was experiencing. Not only was the love of his life killed right before his very eyes, but she died for him! She enlisted in the military for him! And if alive, I bet that she

ᵈ " *Sally St. Clair.*" — Page 87.

Sally St. Clair was a beautiful, dark-eyed, Creole girl. The whole treasury of her love was lavished upon Sergeant Jasper, who on one occasion had the good fortune to save her life. The prospect of their separation almost maddened her. To sever her long jetty ringlets from her exquisite head, to dress in male attire, to enrol herself in the corps to which he belonged, and follow his fortunes in the wars, unknown to him, was a resolution no sooner conceived than taken. In the camp she attracted no particular attention except on the night before the battle, when she was noticed bending over his couch, like a good and gentle spirit, as if listening to his dreams. The camp was surprised and a fierce conflict ensued. The lovers were side by side in the thickest of the fight ; but, endeavouring to turn away a lance aimed at the heart of Jasper, the poor girl received it in her own, and fell bleeding at his feet. After the victory, her name and sex were discovered, and there was not a dry eye in the corps when Sally St. Clair was laid in her grave, near the river Santee, in a green shady nook that looked as if it had been stolen out of Paradise. — *Tales of Marion's Men.*

would have done it all over again. Love is a powerful thing. This is truly one of the most romantic stories I have ever read. Many in the South refer to Sally St. Clair as the Molly Pitcher of the South. Several newspaper articles published in the 1870s stated that Jasper, Sally's lover, did not know she was James St. Clair, the boy soldier. However, that is highly unlikely since Sally was at Jasper's side in every single battle, and they also shared a tent. I'm pretty sure he knew.

"A little rebellion now and then is a good thing."
—Thomas Jefferson

Now, let's discuss the British failed Southern Strategy, shall we? The British military was under the assumption there was a large portion of loyal supporters living in the South who would be glad to join the British militia. The British decided to embark on a Southern Strategy with support from Loyalists in the South. In early 1778, British Secretary Lord George Germain wrote a letter to Sir Henry Clinton, which he stated that *"capturing the Southern colonies was considered by the King as an object of great importance in the scale of the war."* The first plan of action was to take control of the Southern Atlantic port of

Savannah, GA. With control of this port, the British would control imports to Southern plantations and the central mercantile hub. On December 29, 1778, an estimated 2,500 to 3,600 British troops (under the command of General Augustin Prévost), Hessians and Loyalists, captured the city of Savannah, Georgia, with little to no resistance. The Continental Congress decided to take Savannah back. On September 16th, 1779, Patriots, the French, Irishmen, and the Polish all joined General Benjamin Lincoln (Commander of the Southern Army) to launch a plan to take back Savannah, GA, from British occupiers. The French commander Count D'Estaing arrived in early September with twenty ships off the coast of Georgia. The French also had an estimated five hundred French militia and estimated 3,000 to 5,000 French troops aboard the ships, including five hundred Haitians, to assist in the battle. General Prévost sends a message to Colonel Maitland requesting reinforcements, warning him about the arrival of the French fleet. The second Battle of Savannah (1779) will become the most significant foreign contributions in the American Revolutionary War. The Continental Army, militia from South Carolina, regiments from North Carolina, and French allies surrounded the town with cannons, cutting the British off from food supplies. Lincoln asked British commander Prévost, along with an estimate three to two thousand Redcoats from the 71st Regiment and Loyalists, to surrender. Prévost's troops also included the 71st Scottish Highlanders, and Hessian regiments Von Wöllwarth and Von Visum outnumbered the Continental Army by one-half. The British General requested twenty-four hours to think about this proposal; that was a mistake on the allies. Within the twenty-four hours eight hundred British reinforcements arrived. Prévost refused to surrender. For three weeks the Continental Army launched a bombardment of cannon fire on to the town. Even though the cannonballs were aimed at the British occupiers, they sadly killed many civilians (mostly women and children) and only one British soldier.

DEBORAH SAMPSON

I honestly did not want to add this woman soldier to my book; however, I wanted to include all females (names discovered) who dressed as men to fight the battle against tyranny. One of the main reasons I did not want to add her is because she is overexaggerated throughout history as being the only documented female soldier, which by now you can conclude that is not factual. According to the National Women's History Museum, Deborah Sampson was the only woman who received a pension for her participation of the Revolutionary War. Well, let me correct the record. Margaret Corbin was the first female to receive pension (1779) and also received an honorable burial at West Point for her participation in the Revolutionary War. If Deborah Simpson was indeed the first female soldier of the Revolutionary War, don't you think that she would be the one buried at West Point? Deborah received her first pension in 1803. Deborah did have a hard life growing up; she was an indentured servant up until the age of eighteen. She was one of seven children, and when her father abandoned his family and moved to Maine her mother "bound out" (*she "sold"*) her children to other households. Deborah self-educated herself, which is extraordinary on its own. As you will discover, many of these women noted in this book were, in fact, indentured servants and lower-class women.

Deborah enlisted in 1782 as Robert Shirtliff, her deceased brother. Remember, the Revolutionary War ended September 3rd, 1783. So, this woman was only in for

Deborah Sampson as a male soldier and as a lady

one year. Sampson was in the light infantry company of the 4th Massachusetts Regiment. Deborah saw action in 1783, Westchester County, New York, just north of the city of New York, where she was wounded in her thigh and forehead. Because of her injuries, her identity was revealed but kept a secret by a physician. Deborah Sampson was honorably discharged from the Army by Henry Knox. The value of female soldiers is just as priceless as male soldiers. If you wish to learn more about Deborah, the story of her life was written in 1797, by Herman Mann, entitled *The Female Review: or, Memoirs of an American Young Lady.*

CHAPTER 3
Camp Followers

For hundreds of years, large numbers of women and children, merchants, servants, enslaved laborers, and contractors typically accompanied European armies. Most of these women and children were wives and widows of enlisted soldiers, and occasionally those of officers. This tradition carried over to North America. Many Colonial women followed troops to provide support to their husbands, fathers, and brothers who enlisted in the Continental Army to fight in the Revolutionary War. These brave women were called camp followers; these individuals performed domestic duties such as cooking, cleaning, mending uniforms, herding livestock, and foraging for food. They also performed military duties such as reloading cannons and muskets (on and off the battlefield) and tending to ill and injured soldiers. Whenever there was a Continental Army encampment, hundreds of women came into the camps for various reasons. Camp followers' encampments were separated from the Continental Army's and they were not permitted to set up camp next to soldier's tents. Sadly, many historians labeled female camp followers as carrying some fewer appealing attributes, meaning they were prostitutes, as many historians have so narrowly portrayed them. There were prostitutes amongst the camp followers. But that was small in number. To state that all the women who supported the soldiers were prostitutes is appalling. However, for the most part, many camp followers were family members of soldiers in the Army they were following. [97] These brave individuals experienced all the horrors of war. Many camp followers never saw a dead person. Yet by the end of the first battle, they become numb by seeing men die on the battlefield. War would forever change these camp followers, who were not trained as soldiers but were expected to be tough as one. I wonder if they honestly knew what they were getting into. They were experiencing the terror of war, pain, and grief. The American Revolutionary War placed great demands on the colonies, requiring a level of involvement, commitment, and sacrifice unknown to them. Without the steadfast support of the Homefront (camp followers, militiamen, and civilian Patriots), it might have been impossible to secure freedom from King George III. When war erupted, everyday household items were rarely available since many household products came from England.

While the men and boys were away fighting in the campaign, British soldiers would come pillaging through the colonies, violating women, burning crops, and taking whatever they wished.

Historian Alexis Coe states that rape was used as a weapon during the Revolutionary War. In a 2018 interview Coe said the families of raped American women often pointed out that British soldiers maximized the humiliating and demoralizing impact of their attacks by assaulting women in front of their fathers, husbands, and other close relatives. Assaults on the honor of American men who failed to protect their vulnerable women seemed as critical as defeat on the battlefield. This pillaging by the British put the lives of women and children in danger. They were unprotected while the men were away fighting in the war. One could only imagine the fear in a mother's heart when she heard the pounding on her cabin door, yelling, *"Open up, in the name of the king."* That is not to say that these women were incapable of protecting their families. A lot of frontierswomen learned how to hunt and farm.

Rich women, however, were not trained to handle muskets, pistols, and long rifles. The elitists assumed it was not ladylike for a woman to learn how to handle a weapon. Big mistake! Numerous women who were left behind feared for their lives and were afraid that they and their children would not survive the war. Left with no income and few choices, many poor Colonial women thought it wise to become camp followers. Camp followers conducted the duties that soldiers did not want to do. This means that camp followers did women's work, which they widely accepted because the Army offered a measure of safety, security, income, and shelter. Following behind the Continental Army's wagons, camp followers walked in the hot sun in the summer and blistering cold in the winter for miles with their children on their backs or walking alongside them. Camp followers were required to abide by the *Articles of War.* These military laws governed the Army; if they did not, they could be beaten or drummed out of the camp, which meant dishonorable dismissal from military service.

Source: William S. Leney

The Soldier's Wife

Yale Center for British Art, Paul Mellon Collection

Most camp followers were poor farmers with no shoes, and their clothing was nothing but dirty rags. Camp followers engaged in the service of the Continental Army when America was at war (definition of an auxiliary person). According to the United States Army support personnel (auxiliary) assist the military or police but are organized differently from regular forces. Auxiliary may be military volunteers undertaking support functions or performing certain duties such as garrison troops. An estimated four thousand women were considered "on the strength." So, in other words, camp followers were officially part of the military and able to draw half-rations per day and receive payment.[98] Therefore, the Continental Army and the British Army were much larger than historians assumed. Not every individual employed in an army is an infantry soldier. Many noncombative roles must be filled within a military force. Commander-in-Chief George Washington dealt directly with Army troops within the camps, during troop movements and on and off the battlefields. Within his general orders, there are several instances where he commented on the women following the Army. August 4, 1777, Washington drafted general Orders at Colonel Hills' headquarters in Roxboro, Massachusetts. The Orders stated:

> *...the multitude of women in particular, especially those who are pregnant, or have children, are a clog upon every movement—The Commander in Chief therefore earnestly recommends it, to the officers commanding brigades and corps, to use every reasonable method in their power, to get rid of all such as are not absolutely necessary; and the admission or continuance of any, who shall, or may have come to the Army since its arrival in Pennsylvania, is positively forbidden; to which point the officers will give particular attention.* [99]

Wives of officers did not travel behind the Army as did other camp followers. Instead, they enjoyed the luxuries of a cabin and better provisions. Talk about privilege! Martha Washington spent every winter with her husband in the camp of the Continental Army. She performed many of the tasks that other camp followers performed.[100] However, it was in the luxury of being in a warm environment

Source: *The Camp Followers,* by Wilhelm Diez (1888)

versus the other camp followers that were outside in the cold doing laundry and cooking. American historian Carol Berkin stated in her book *Revolutionary Mothers* that history books about the American Revolutionary War are primarily written about the generals and nobles like Patrick Henry. Berkin also noted that women's whereabouts were not included in history books until the 1980s. I would argue that in today's world (21st century) women are still rarely mentioned in new publications regarding Revolutionary War history. As the war progressed, General Washington recognized the value that camp women contributed to the Army and exhorted his men to treat the women as ***regular Army personnel***. However, the Continental Congress disagreed with Washington's tone toward camp followers. The Continental Congress stated in the Articles of War defined camp followers as retainers to a camp and all persons whatsoever serving with the armies who were not soldiers.[101] Well, in the twenty-first century, the Department of Defense (DOD) would agree with General Washington. The DOD would view camp followers as part of Operational Readiness, a vital aspect of defense logistics. [102] And what does that mean? It means that camp followers were part of the Continental Army military force and should be recognized as military personnel. Something that historians failed to connect. But not this rookie historian. These camp followers assisted the Continental Army soldiers in being ready for battles. They properly maintained weapons and supplies (supply specialists), administered emergency medical care in the field (medics), and provided food (Army culinary specialists) and cares for the soldiers so they may properly function. Washington eventually recognized the value of women in the camps. Women were very much involved on the battlefields. They molded bullets, carried gunpowder to the soldiers, loaded pistols and muskets, carried water to swab the artillery barrels, gave water to thirsty troops, and fired cannons. Camp followers also provided frontline trauma care and dragged the injured off the battlefields while under enemy fire. These were brave women! A significant number of women were killed by enemy fire when attending to their duties on the battlefield. We can only imagine what these women and children witnessed while watching and participating on the battlefield. Watching men die, possibly their fathers, brothers, or husbands. The anguish and fear they must have experienced while witnessing intimate violence. Children must have been frightened the first time they heard cannons go off and the cries of men fighting in battle. These women and children were exposed to many different traumatic events, which would most likely affect them for the rest of their lives. A sad and long-lasting trauma of war.

Discipline for camp followers was harsh. For example, women caught fornicating with a man other than her husband would be sentenced to fifty lashes in full view of her company and cast out, never to be a camp follower with that company again. While on marches, camp followers, which also included elderly men and runaway children, walked at the column's rear with the baggage. If a horse or oxen were too weak to pull the loads, the women were expected to pull or push the wagons.[103] Once a campsite was approved for the evening, the camp followers unloaded the heavy cooking equipment, set up a makeshift kitchen and prepared the evening's meal.

Women and their older children would tend to the campfires after the soldiers turned in for the night. Women and children who were in charge of cooking would also be up at the crack of dawn preparing and serving breakfast.

C | Cook's Regiment. | **R. I.**

Mary Carl

Appears as signature to a

Receipt Roll

of which the following is a copy:

"We the Subcribers whose Names are under written have Received of Cornelius Briggs the Whole of our Bounty which was Due from the first Day of August 1778 to 26 Day of August 1778 for the Rhode Island Expidishon I Say Received by me—"

(Revolutionary War.)

Roll dated *Little Compton*

April 30., 1779.

Remarks:

Number of record

1   *L. Morrison*

(545i)   Copyist.

Example of a camp follower's military service record. Many women were paid for their services, so that means they were part of the Continental Army military force.

Source: U.S. Complied Revolutionary War, Military Service Records, 1775-1783

When it was time to march to the next destination, it was the women who dismantled the kitchens, packed the wagons, gathered the children, hitched, and harnessed the draft animals, and then again fell in at the end of the column for the day's march.[104]

Average Colonial women could not read or write. Education was only fit for a man. Now, this does not mean that many women did not self-educate. These women had plenty of common sense. For example, they knew that you would have to boil white oak bark to treat tonsilitis, and for laxatives you would use a Senna leaf. Collectively, female camp followers were known as Mollies. For example, Molly Hays, whose real name was Mary Ludwig Hays, courageously fought in the battle of Monmouth on June 28, 1778. Mary would also be called Molly Pitcher. Please note, this is very important—the name Molly Pitcher is a collective generic term inasmuch as "G.I. Joe" was a moniker for an American soldier. The name Molly Pitcher, like the term G.I. Joe, is a common label for the countless nameless women who are not honored for their heroic service. Because no one individual can be accurately identified as Molly, many women qualify to be called by what has come to be the honorary title of Molly Pitcher. Many historians consider "Molly Pitcher" to be most closely linked with Mary Ludwig Hays. With this story having many comparisons to Margaret Corbin's story in addition to her nickname of Captain Molly, it is no surprise that she too was often called Molly Pitcher. Unfortunately, the name Molly Pitcher has led to misunderstanding causing the historical details about these women's roles to become comingled and mythologized.[105] Because many of these camp followers were only known by the name Molly, it would suggest the majority these women's real names are forever lost in history.

In early 1775, a request was made by General Horatio Gates to General Washington to have women camp followers care for his wounded soldiers. Washington, in turn, asked Congress for funds for nurses to attend the sick. A plan was formulated to provide one nurse for every ten patients and one matron for every one hundred wounded or ill soldiers. This became the first instance of an organized nursing system in the military. Congress allowed a salary of $2.00 per month for these nurses; matrons were allotted $4.00 per month with complete food rations.[106] Many of them never saw the money. Remember, women were the property of their fathers and husbands. When they were paid, the money went to their husband or father. If a camp follower's husband or father is *hors de combat* (killed in action), they had the opportunity to be remarried. If not, they were ordered home. To provide a means for caring for sick soldiers, Congress authorized the formation of hospitals. Washington asked his commanding officers to assist regimental surgeons in procuring as many women of the Army (camp followers) as could be prevailed on to serve as nurses who would be paid the usual price. Hold up, wait a minute, did Washington just admit in writing that women were part of the Army? I think so! Later, after the reorganization of the Continental Army medical staff, one hospital matron and ten nurses were allocated for every hundred sick and wounded men.[107] Being in a more supervisory position, the matrons got 50 cents a day plus the full ratio. According to Thomas E. Devoe, in an article published in 1981 called "The Women of the Camp," one female camp follower was assigned to every forty to seventy men.[108]

In Walter Blumenthal's landmark 1952 study, *Women Camp Followers of the American Revolution,* he attempts to calculate the number of women who followed specific regiments. Because the British held the distinction of maintaining the highest number of camp followers with a ratio of women to men at one to eight, Blumenthal's estimated the number of camp followers in British General John Burgoyne's army at about one thousand women to eight thousand men. [109] Wow, that's a lot. These numbers may not be exact; however, it gives the notion of how many camp followers contributed to the eighteenth-century Army. Perhaps given that camp followers in the American Revolutionary War were taken for granted, an adequate account of the women and children might never be accurate. Among the American forces, Blumenthal theorized that camp followers were fewer in number because of the shortage of food and the inability of the Continental Army to sustain them. According to Washington's orders, the proportion of women in the camps did not exceed a ratio of one per thirteen men.[110] In contrast, Blumenthal's study of camp followers fails to recognize that the chief motivation to follow the armies was not romantic adventure but resulted from the war itself. Blumenthal stated that women followed the Continental Army for romantic reasons. One of the more colorful narratives about camp followers that describes their desperate condition is that of Hannah Winthrop. She had watched as Burgoyne's troops marched through Boston and wrote to her friend Mercy Otis Warren about this spectacle. On November 11th, 1777, her letter says:

> *To be sure the sight was truly astonishing. I never had the least idea that the Creation produced such a sordid set of creatures in human Figure—poor, dirty, emaciated men, great numbers of women, who seemed to be the beasts of burthen having a bushel basket on their back, by which they were bent double, the contents seemed to be Pots and kettles, various sorts of furniture, children Peeping thro' gridirons and other utensils, some very young infants who were Born on the road, the woman bare feet, cloathed in dirty rags, such effluvia filled the air while they were passing, had they not been smoking all the time, I should have been apprehensive of being contaminated by them.*[111]

It is scarce for history books to place women in a masculine role (i.e., warrior). While conducting historical research, it was discovered that history books gave more credit to a female's husband's achievements than elaborating on the female's contribution to history and the war. History should reflect that these women were part of the Continental Army versus being a burden. For hundreds of years, these women were dismissed because of gender bias. Yes, that's right, I said it. Women are underrepresented, misrepresented, and ostracized in history textbooks when it comes to writing about wars. Historically, history books pertaining to women are written about their stereotypically domestic duties and are romanticized by published letters they wrote to their husbands or lovers. Let this book correct that theory.

> *"There was one of two things I had a right to: liberty or death. If I could not have one, I would take the other, or no man should take me alive. I should fight for liberty as long as my strength lasted." – Harriet Tubman*

Source: Image courtesy of Library of Congress, Prints and Photographs Division, Washington, D.C.

This is the only known depiction of a woman camp follower in a period image of the Continental Army. Thousands of women and children, however, shared life on campaign with their enlisted husbands and fathers. A census of the camp followers at West Point in January 1782 documents the presence of 150 women and 91 children alongside about 3,600 soldiers. The woman seen here is holding a tin kettle while two soldiers use their spoons to eat directly from the pot.[112]

"As a society, we should recreate the voice of the
inaccurate past historical events and
give life to those who are overlooked and viewed as inferior."
- Juanita Stellato Maldonado

MARGARET COCHRAN CORBIN

There were warrior-like women like Margaret Cochran Corbin, who was also known as Captain Molly. Margaret decided to answer the door when war started knocking. Margaret was born in 1751 and was 5 foot 8 inches tall. [113] It is suspected that she is of Scottish descent. In 1758, her father was killed by the Indians and her mother was taken prisoner. By the time 1765 rolled around she had not heard from her mother, so she and the rest of her siblings were placed under the guardianship of their maternal uncle. Margaret married John Corbin in 1772, who later enlisted in the 1st Pennsylvania Artillery in 1775. Margaret chose to follow her husband's unit as a camp follower. It was better than being left alone in Pennsylvania. Dr. Debra Michals's essay (1999) noted that the hardships of Corbin's young life inspired the courage and resilience that would serve her well during the Revolution.[114] Margaret fought in the Battle of Fort Washington, which took place in New York on November 16, 1776. Fort Washington was the last American stronghold in New York. General William Howe was caught up in the romantic idea that he would be the one to defeat George Washington. General Howe defeated Washington and his troops at the Battle of White Plains in October. That is when Howe started to focus his attention on Fort Washington. Washington was at Fort Lee when Howe decided to attack Fort Washington. With Washington being at Fort Lee, he mistakenly left Fort Washington unprotected, even though Washington ordered General Nathanael Greene to defend the fort. Here's a fun fact: Fort Washington and Fort Lee (Battle of Fort Lee: November 19, 1776) are directly across the river from each other. I suspect Washington was watching the chaos happen.

Turncoat William Dumont, who defected to the British unbeknownst to General Washington, provided the British with the blueprints of Fort Washington. With the information provided by the turncoat, Howe launched a three-pronged assault. His troops (British and Hessians, 8,000 strong) stormed the fort from the North, East, and South. In the beginning, the Patriots gave a good fight. However, the numbers were against them, and unfortunately the Patriots (3,000 strong) had to retreat into the safety of the fort. Since the Patriots decided to revert back to the fort, overcrowding happened and Colonel McGaw had no choice but to surrender. If only that turncoat did not turn over the blueprints, perhaps the Americans

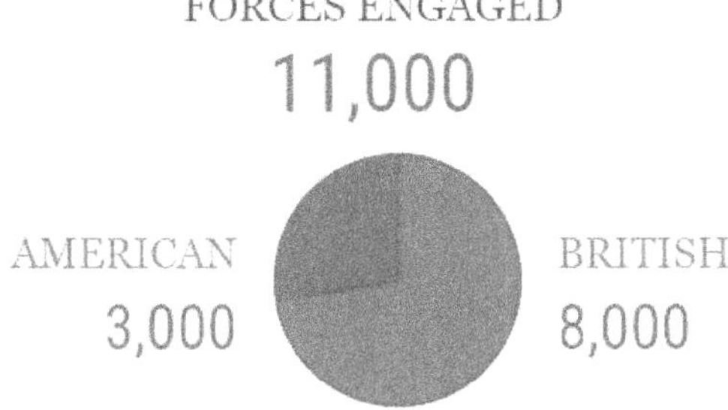

ESTIMATED CASUALTIES
613

AMERICAN
155

BRITISH
458

Source: American Battlefield Trust

would have won. The British took 2,800 prisoners and commandeered Fort Washington's weapons and provisions. The estimated casualties were a total of:

During the Battle of Fort Washington, Hessian soldiers were pushed back several times by fire from the cannons. As the battle ensued, a gunner was killed. John Corbin took over his firing while his wife, Margaret, took over as matross on top of Forest Hill. In the heat of the battle, Margaret witnessed her husband killed (it is unknown how he died). Without hesitation, Margaret heroically continued to fire the cannons against the British. Fellow soldiers called Margaret "Captain Molly," who had a steady aim and sure shot. Like a true Patriot, she stepped up and did not hesitate or calculate the dangers she might face. Honestly, she already knew. She was a camp follower and frequently followed her husband into different battles. In battle, you run the risk of being shot or even killed. Captain Molly did not permit these thoughts to enter her mind. The cannon fire did not stop the Hessian or British soldiers from gaining an advantage in taking the hill. Soon Captain Molly was hit, in her left arm (nearly severing it), her jaw, and her left breast, leaving her severely wounded.[115] While both sides were walking the battleground—some as victors, the other as prisoners of war—they were surprised when they witnessed a young woman sitting beside the cannon and her dead husband (John Corbin). The soldiers noticed Margaret's injured arm, which was hanging by a tendon, and her chest nearly crushed. According to historian Debra Michals, Ph.D., Corbin dressed as a man and joined her husband in the battlefield.[116] On September 15, the British captured New York City.[117] Historian Linda Grant De Pauw describes Margaret Corbin as a transvestite soldier who wore a uniform but made no attempt to conceal her sex. [118] The National Women's History Museum also backs up this claim.[119] Margaret enlisting and dressing as a man is largely excluded when historians discuss her adventures or her participation in the Battle of Fort Washington. You would think in the 21st century that women's history would be written correctly. However, when I pick up a world-renowned or bestseller history book relating to Revolutionary War battles, I never read the names of the women noted in this book. And when I say never, I mean never. The only books pertaining to these women are children's romantic novels (historical fiction) and books published in the 1700s.

Usually when images are depicting Margaret, she is wearing a Colonial dress loading a cannon versus her in a man's uniform with her hair flowing down. I guess historians wish not to make her masculine. During their three years with the Continental Army, John and Margaret's duty was a matross; his job was to assist artillery gunners in loading, sponging, firing, and moving the guns. John mostly sponged out and loaded the cannons.

Captain Molly was taken prisoner and Colonel Robert Magaw, commanding officer, surrendered, giving the British a decisive victory. Captain Molly was counted amongst the prisoners who were released back to the care of the Revolutionary hospitals. Half of General Greene's army was captured at the Battle of Fort Washington. The Hudson River (also known as the No Man's Land) falls in the hands of the British; this battle depleted the morale of the Continental Army. Many wondered if the military might of Great Britain could truly be defeated. We must remember that when the flames of Patriotism are ignited, they will never go out until the last soldier's dying breath.

Source: Ten American Girls from History, by Kate Dickinson Sweetser
Margaret Cochran loading the cannon

Three days after the fall of Fort Washington, General Washington abandoned Fort Lee and retreated toward the Delaware River, which would become the site of his iconic crossing of the Delaware into the Battle of Trenton (December 26, 1776). Don't worry, I talk about that battle later in the book. Shortly after British commandeered Fort Washington, the American forces learned of Demont's treason. However, General Washington kept it under wraps because he didn't want to further damage the morale of his troops. Personally, I would have sent out a militia to hunt him down to be executed in public. But that's just me.

Once Captain Molly recovered (meaning did not die) from her debilitating wounds, which left her unable to use her left arm for the rest of her life, she was reassigned to the Pennsylvania Corps of Invalid as a private soldier, at West Point, where she aided the wounded until she was formerly discharged in 1783. Why don't you read that sentence again? She was reassigned as a private soldier. Officially! Her name appears on the discharge rolls of the Invalid Regiment Rolls of 1783. Captain Molly decided to remain in the neighborhood of West Point. After all, the poor woman had no relatives or close ties anywhere else; one place was just as good as another.

After Margaret Corbin's discharge, Quartermaster William Price, Deputy Commissary of Military Stores, took it upon himself to care for Margaret. Price reported to General Henry Knox, Secretary at War. Price grew overly concerned pertaining to Margaret's debilitating combat wounds. He wrote several letters to General Henry Knox. Price writes in one of his letters:

Enclosed is an account of Mrs. Elizabeth Simms for taking care of Capt. Molly twelve weeks, as the Bearer will return you and forward the money by him—I am at a loss what to do with Capt. Molly. She is first an offensive person that people are unwilling to take her in charge, this woman informs me that she cannot keep her longer than the first of March, and I cannot any that is willing to keep her for that money and find her everything to eat and drink—if you should think proper to extend one or two rations to her and will be better than money and may induce some person to keep her."[120]

Another letter written in 1787 states that an American regiment stationed at West Point enclosed receipts showing fourteen pounds 8/ is for taking care of Captain Molly for 24 weeks, twelve of which were from October 26th, 1785, to January 18th, 1786, inclusively. The other twelve are from July 6 to September 27th, 1786, inclusive as receipts will show all the above receipts as depicted. At least they were trying to take care of Margaret. I believe that she became aggressive because she had experienced trauma while being in combat and was severely wounded, as well as witnessing her husband dying on the battlefield. The poor woman probably experienced flashbacks, nightmares, severe anxiety, and uncontrollable aggression related to Post-Traumatic Stress Disorder, known as PTSD. Many individuals who have never experienced war trauma could not connect to Margaret and her pain, both physically and mentally. So, therefore, she was not understood by the civilian community.

On July 6, 1779, the Continental Congress resolved that Captain Molly heroically filled the post of her husband, who was killed by her side, that she do receive, during her natural life or the continuance of the said disability, the one-half of the monthly pay drawn by a soldier in the service of these states; and that she now receive out of the public stores one complete suit of clothes, or the value thereof in money.[121] Margaret Corbin is the first American female to receive a soldier's lifetime pension after the Revolutionary War. However, historical literature would have you believe that Deborah Simpson was the first female American Revolutionary War soldier who disguised herself as a man to receive a full military

Source: Plaque honoring Corbin on Margaret Corbin Drive in Fort Tryon Park

pension or participation as a soldier in the Revolutionary Army. Deborah received her pension in 1803. [122] Let the record be corrected.

The Continental Army recognized Captain Molly as a steady soldier and regarded her as such. Her regiment petitioned successfully for Corbin to receive both State and Federal pensions the same year she was discharged; however, she was not awarded her pension until 1779.[123]

Captain Molly died at the age of forty-eight on January 16, 1800, in Highland Falls, New York, as a result of her war injuries. In 1926, her remains were removed and relocated to West Point's Old Cadet Chapel. The body's identity was verified by doctors who examined the corpse and noticed the body had damage done to the arm, chest, and jaw during confirming that this was indeed Margaret's remains. Because Margaret was a member of Active Duty at West Point, there is a treasure trove of primary sources such as documentation located at the U.S. Military Academy Cemetery, West Point, New York, correspondence letters from her commanding officer at West Point, and secondary sources from History of American Women blogs, published essays all containing vital information regarding her time served in the American Revolutionary War.[124]

Many historians have gotten the story of Margaret wrong. Some say she never fired a cannon before the battle at Fort Washington. However, it was known

Source: Daughters of the American Revolution, 1926, newspaper article,
the only monument to a woman veteran on the grounds of West Point

that in most of the battles her husband participated in, she also helped man the cannons. It was not uncommon for a camp follower to man the cannons. Also, several historians depict Margaret as the average Colonial woman wearing a dress and having her hair up while shooting a cannon when she was dressed as a man. You will see Margaret's name if you ever pick up the *Encyclopedia of American Women at War from the Home Front to the Battlefields,* by Lisa Tendrick Frank. However, two sentences are only contributed to this woman. Heroines, in my book, are largely overlooked by historical literature. Courageous women and men should be written about without the author being discriminatory based on one's sex or gender.

"Margaret proved how brave a woman could be.
And just because we are women does not necessarily mean
we cannot be as courageous as men."
—Juanita Stellato Maldonado

MARY LUDWIG HAYS

Mary was born to German immigrants on January 4, 1742. Some historians claim she was born in New Jersey, others in Pennsylvania. However, on the DAR website it shows that she was born in Charles, Cumberland County, Pennsylvania (with no supporting evidence). I discovered Mary Ludwig (or Ludwick, as noted on her marriage record) Hays while researching through the online *National Archives.* I found a piece written in 1999 by Emily J. Teipe. She states, *"Mary was described by the men in her company as a twenty-two-year-old illiterate pregnant woman who smoked and chewed tobacco and swore and any of the male soldiers."* I do not know about you, but Mary sounds like a fun person to be around. So, I started to research about this person I never heard of. A 1928 newspaper article stated that Mary was also an indentured servant (age sixteen). A woman named Anna Callender, wife to William Irvine, served as a brigadier General in the Continental Army. Mrs. Callender took an interest in young Mary and so decided to purchase her for domestic work. Mary was not an indentured servant; she was not paying off any debt. She was purchased as a slave.

Mary had two husbands. The first was William "John" Casper Hays (Irish), whom she married in 1769. John enlisted in 1769 and was assigned to Captain Thomas Proctor's 4th Continental Artillery Regiment, also known as Reign's Continental Artillery Regiment (Pennsylvania Artillery). He was an artilleryman and, some historians say, a gunner. When her first husband enlisted in the Continental Army, Mary remained with her master. In 1777 John re-enlisted in the 7th Pennsylvania Regiment, Continental line in a company commanded by Captain John Alexander. Mary decided to meet her husband instead of living with her mother. It is unclear on how Mary gained her freedom from Mrs. Callender. Mary's husband missed her terribly and sent word where she could find him and to become a camp follower.

Mary accompanied her husband at the battle of Fort Clinton, October 6, 1777, where unfortunately the British General Henry Clinton gained victory by dividing their troops to stage simultaneous attacks on Fort Clinton and Fort Montgomery. The purpose of this attack on Fort Clinton and Montgomery is that the British wanted to create a diversion to gain control of the Hudson River. Both fortifications had a total of fifty cannons. The British bombarded both forts with cannon fire; they also landed 2,000 (some say 4,000) troops on the west bank under heavy fog to launch their assault on forts Montgomery and Clinton. The British moved inland, dividing their forces; half of the British forces attacked the rear of Fort Montgomery while the remaining troops attacked Fort Clinton. Governor and General George Clinton (no relation to the British General) sends urgent word to General Putnam across the river requesting assistance. There were only 600 New York State militia stationed at both forts. The Local American militia placed a chain (Hudson River Chain) that stretched across the river to prevent any British ships from sailing further north. In the heat of the battle, Mary's husband dropped his match and field to the cannon. Mary picked it up and fired! That was the last cannon fired from Fort Clinton.[125] The Hudson River was a valuable strategic location for both the British and the Continental Army. Whoever controlled the Hudson River controlled the future of the war. Fort Clinton was located near the Hudson River Valley not far from West Point, south of New York Harbor. General James Clinton ordered his New York militia to retreat through Popolopen Gorge Creek. Casualties were high on the American side; they lost half of their men. Once the British took over both fortifications they burned them to the ground to counteract the movement of the British on New York. Once again, Washington marched his troops into New Jersey (first time was December 25, 1776; General Washington boldly led his men across the icy Delaware River and on a ten-mile march into Trenton, New Jersey, where they surprised a garrison of 1,500 Hessians).

At the battle of Monmouth (June 28, 1778) the British forces were an estimated 15,000 strong, and the Continental Army only had 11,000 troops. General Washington ordered General Charles Lee (who commanded the advance guard) to attack the British rear. When General Lee attempted to surround the small force at the courthouse, he was surprised by the arrival of General Cornwallis' rearguard, which General Clinton had ordered back to resist the attackers. General Lee ordered a retreat; however, he did not inform Washington right away. When Washington arrived at the battle, he was surprised to find his army retreating. Let's say that Washington was a little pissed off. He re-formed his men to delay until his following units were in a battle line. There were attacks

COMMANDERS

AMERICAN
George
Washington

BRITISH
Charles
Cornwallis

FORCES ENGAGED
26,000

AMERICAN
11,000

BRITISH
15,000

ESTIMATED CASUALTIES
1,300

AMERICAN
600

BRITISH
700

Source: American Battlefield Trust

and counterattacks by both sides throughout the scorching afternoon. General Clinton rested his men until midnight, then he retreated to the coast and was evacuated by the Royal Navy. Washington did not waste his time following the British. Both sides claimed victory. However, history recorded it as inconclusive. General Washington marched his troops to the Hudson River to join the Continental Army, while General Clinton's forces returned to New York.

While the battle was in progress, Mary carried water from a neighboring spring, back and forth. She went while under fire, supplying the much-needed water to men on the battlefield, hence her being recognized as a Molly Pitcher because she carried a pitcher from the well to the soldiers. While rushing water to the soldiers, she discovered John Hays was injured in battle (however, some historians state he suffered from heat exhaustion). Mary took his place at the cannon, performing skillfully and heroically. Like so many other Patriots, tradition states that she received the personal thanks of General Washington and was commissioned as a non-commissioned officer. Sadly, her husband John died from his wounds sustained from the battle. There are several versions of this story as well. Either George Washington merely complimented Mary Hayes, thanked her, or bestowed some reward. Author Walter Blumenthal states that Washington gave Mary a gold piece and promoted her to sergeant for her bravery during the Battle of Monmouth; however, there is no evidence in the military records of her having been promoted. An old Revolutionary rhyme tells the story of Mary: *"Molly Pitcher she stood by her gun, and rammed the charges home, sir, and thus on Monmouth's bloody field a sergeant did become, Sir."*

MOLLY PITCHER*

[June 23, 1778]

LAURA ELIZABETH RICHARDS

All day the great guns barked and roared;
All day the big balls screeched and soared;
All day, 'mid the sweating gunners grim,
Who toiled in their smoke-shroud dense and dim,
Sweet Molly labored with courage high,
With steady hand and watchful eye,
Till the day was ours, and the sinking sun
Looked down on the field of Monmouth won,
And Molly standing beside her gun.

Now, Molly, rest your weary arm!
Safe, Molly, all is safe from harm.
Now, woman, bow your aching head,
And weep in sorrow o'er your dead!

Next day on that field so hardly won,
Stately and calm stands Washington,
And looks where our gallant Greene doth lead
A figure clad in motley weed —

Source: "Molly Pitcher" by Laura Elizabeth Richards

Many historic literatures published regarding these battles mentioned, failed to include Mary. And if they do mention her, she has one or two sentences out of an entire book dedicated to her. Many early historians claim that there is absolutely no evidence of Mary's heroic deeds in battle. This is just a legend conjured up for the troops' morale; however, her service record and place as a historical figure are also validated by the documentation of one eyewitness at the Battle of Monmouth; Private Joseph Plumb Martin substantiates that Molly Pitcher (Mary Ludwick) was more than just a legend. In Mr. Martin's memoirs, published in 1830, he stated the following:

> *A woman whose husband belonged to the artillery and who was then attached to a piece in the engagement attended with her husband at the piece the whole time. While in the act of reaching [for] a cartridge and having one of her feet as far before the other as she could step, a cannon shot from the enemy passed directly between her legs without doing any other damage than carrying away all the lower part of her petticoat. Looking at it with apparent unconcern, she observed that it was lucky it did not pass a little higher, for in that case it might have carried away something else, and continued her occupation.*[126]

Mr. Martin states that Mary Ludwig Hayes appeared on Captain Thomas Proctor's company, Pennsylvania Artillery, roster war record on June 28, 1778, to serve for two years.

In a 1927 book titled *The Battle of Monmouth*, William Stryker quotes the diary of a surgeon named Albigence Waldo, who had heard a similar story from a wounded soldier he treated at the battle. The woman had taken up her fallen husband's gun and *"like a Spartan heroine"* she *"fought with astonishing bravery, discharging the piece with as much regularity as any soldier present."* Albigence Waldo (1750-94) was an Army surgeon whose diary from the 1777-1778 winter survives Waldo's diary entry for July 3, 1778. While Dr. Waldo kept a well-organized diary of his time at Valley Forge the preceding winter, the

Source: Monmouth County Historical Association

volume from the above passage has apparently been lost to history. After Mary Ludwig Hays' heroic deeds during the Battle of Monmouth, she was forever known as Sergeant Molly.

On February 21, 1822, the State of Pennsylvania awarded her with an annual pension of forty dollars ($778 in 2020) for her heroism at Monmouth.

Mary's second husband was a fellow named George McCauley. She married him after her first husband, John Casper Hays, died. She is one of three women to receive a pension for her service (Pennsylvania State Archives, RG-2.60). So there you go, folks; you have one firsthand account witness testimony, a surgeon's testimony from a patient at the battle, and Pennsylvania legislature granting her a pension for Mary's heroic deeds in the Battle of Monmouth. After the American Revolutionary War was over Mary returned to Carlisle, Pennsylvania, to work as a servant.[127] Fun fact: Margaret Corbin served in the same artillery regiment as Mary Ludwig Hayes. I wonder if they knew each other.

Mary died with full military honors on January 22nd, 1832. Spouses of soldiers are not buried with full military honors, even a General's spouse. She was buried at the old cemetery east of South Hanover Street in Carlisle. Mary "Molly" Ludwig Hays McCauley was originally buried in an unmarked grave in Carlisle. A stone marker was placed in the Old Public Graveyard in 1876, and the bronze memorial, sculpted by J. Otto Schweizer of Philadelphia, was erected in 1916.

Her obituary reads:

> Died on Sunday last, Mrs. Mary McAuley (better known by the name of Molly McAuley), aged about 90 years. The history of this woman is somewhat remarkable. Her first husband's name was Hays, who was a soldier in the war of the Revolution. It appears that she continued with him while in the army, and acted so much the part of a heroine, as to attract the notice of the officers. Some estimate may be formed of the value of the service rendered by her, when the fact is stated that she drew a pension from the government during the latter years of her life.

"When the government violates the people's rights, insurrection is,
for the people and for each portion of the people,
the most sacred of the rights and the most indispensable of duties."
—General Marquis La Fayette

SARAH OSBORN BENJAMIN

Sarah Matthews was born in London, England, in 1714. Sarah had a total of five children and outlived each one. However, some historians state that she was born November 17th, 1745, in Orange County, New York, and that she was married three times instead of twice. Let us try to solve this mystery, shall we? My research shows that Sarah was a servant in a blacksmith's household in Albany, New York, when in 1780 she met and married Aaron Osborn. Her new husband reenlisted in the Continental Army (without informing her, the nerve of him) under Captain James Gregg's Co., in a regiment commanded by Colonel Peter Gansevoort, then called the 3rd New York Reg't.[128] Sarah declined to join her husband, that is until she was informed by Captain Gregg that her husband should be put on the commissary guard and that she should have the means of conveyance either in a wagon or on horseback. So she accompanied her husband and the forces under command of Captain Gregg on the east side of the Hudson River to Fishkill, then crossed the river and went down to West Point. They moved on to Williamsburg, remaining two days till the Army all came in by land and then marched for Yorktown, or Little York, as it was then called. After two years of serving with Captain James' regiment, he was transferred to another regiment commanded by Colonel Goose Van Schaick.

Sarah worked as a washerwoman, cook, and nurse, and performed garrison duties on at least one occasion. Sarah, accompanied by her said husband and the same forces, returned during the same season to West Point. Sarah recollects no other females in company but the wife of Lieutenant Forman and of Sergeant Lamberson. According to a newspaper article by the *Scrantonian Tribune* in Pennsylvania, published in 1956, one night while Sarah's first husband was on century duty he was completely overcome with fatigue. To fall asleep at one's post was then and now an unforgivable offense. Sarah, undertaking the situation at once, took his heavy cape and gun and stood Sentinel in his place. It so happened that General Washington was in the area at the time and conducted a walkthrough. When he came upon Sarah standing bravely at her husband's post. Washington, asked, *"Who puts you here?"* Sarah replied in her not-too-perfect grammar, *"Them that had a right to."* No further explanation was necessary for Washington.[129]

In November 1837, Sarah personally appeared before the Court of Common Pleas of Wayne County, PA, at the age of 81 years to give her sworn testimony, in order to obtain the benefit of the provision made by the act of Congress, passed July 4, 1836, and the act explanatory of said act, passed March 3, 1837. [130] In other words, a pension request.

Her testimony:

> *Captain Gregg's regiment arrived at Yorktown in October 1781 (near the end of the battel, it started in September). The New York troops were posted at the right, the Connecticut troops next, and the French to the left. In about one day or less than a day, they reached the place of encampment about one mile from Yorktown. I was on foot and the other females above named and her said husband still on the commissary's guard. My attention was arrested by the appearance of a large plain between them and Yorktown and an entrenchment thrown up. I also saw a number of dead Negroes lying round their encampment, whom I understood the British had driven out of the town and left to starve, or were first starved and then thrown out. I took my stand just back of the American tents, say about a mile from the town, and busied myself with washing, mending, and cooking for the soldiers, in which she I assisted by the other females; some men washed their own clothing. I heard the roar of the artillery for a number of days, and the last night the Americans threw up entrenchments, it was a misty, foggy night, rather wet but not rainy. Every soldier threw up for himself, as I understood, and I afterwards saw and went into the entrenchments. My said husband was there throwing up entrenchments, and I cooked and carried in beef, and bread, and coffee (in a gallon pot) to the soldiers in the entrenchment.*

Sarah was regarded as the *Angel of Mercy*. She attended to a great number of wounded soldiers, mending their horrible battle wounds, comforting them as they cried out in pain. On one occasion when Sarah was thus employed carrying in provisions, she met General Washington (again), who asked her if she was not afraid of the cannonballs. She replied, *"No, the bullets would not cheat the gallows.... It would not do for the men to fight and starve too."* The Continental Army dug entrenchments nearer and nearer to Yorktown every night or two till the last. While digging that, the enemy fired very heavy till about nine o'clock next morning, then stopped, and the drums from the enemy beat excessively. Sarah was a little way off in Colonel Van Schaick's or the officers' marquee and a number of officers were present, among whom was Captain Gregg who, on account of infirmities, did not go out much to do duty. The drums continued beating, and all at once the officers hurrahed and swung their hats, and Sarah asked them, *"What is the matter now?"* One of them replied, *"Are not you soldier enough to know what it means?"* Sarah replied, *"No."* They then replied, *"The British have surrendered."* Sarah, having provisions ready, carried the same down to the entrenchments that morning, and four of the soldiers she was in the habit of cooking for ate their breakfasts.

Sarah stood on one side of the road and the American officers upon the other side when the British officers came out of the town and rode up to the American officers and delivered up (their swords). Sarah thought they returned again, and the British officers rode right on before the Army, who marched out beating and playing a melancholy tune, their drums covered with black handkerchiefs and their fifes with black ribbands tied around them into an old field, and there they grounded their arms and then returned into town again to await their destiny. Sarah recollects seeing a great many American officers, some on horseback and some on foot, but cannot call them all by name. Washington, Lafayette, and Clinton were among the number. The British General at the head of the Army was a large, portly man, full face, and the tears rolled down his cheeks as he passed along. She does not recollect his name, but it was not Cornwallis. She saw the latter afterwards and noticed his being a man of diminutive appearance and having crossed eyes.

Ongoing into town, she noticed two dead Negroes lying by the market house. She had the curiosity to go into a large building that stood nearby, and there she noticed the cupboards smashed to pieces and china dishes and other ware strewed around upon the floor, and among the rest a pewter cover to a hot basin that had a handle on it. She picked it up, supposing it to belong to the British, but the governor came in and claimed it as his but said he would have the name of giving it away, as it was the last one out of twelve that he could see and accordingly presented it to Sarah. Afterwards she brought it home with her to Orange County and sold it for old pewter, which she has a hundred times regretted.

Sarah spent about three years in the military, during which time she had two children, Phoebe and Aaron Jr. Living with the troops, Sarah must have been a rather pathetic sight. While encamped with her husband and family near Philadelphia, some Quaker ladies visiting the camp took pity on her, urged her to leave, and offered her asylum. Sarah explained to them that she could not because of her husband's refusal to leave her behind when the Army resumed march. After discharge, she and her husband stayed near their last encampment at New Windsor, New York (near West Point). Shortly thereafter, her husband abandoned her and the children. That is correct—after all she did for him, he abandoned her. Awesome. Sarah heard rumors that he had taken residence near Newburgh, New York, with another woman. She went there to confront him and discovered that he had married a young woman named Polly Sloat. What a schmuck! Sarah returned to Blooming Grove in Orange County, New York, where she met and married her second husband, a Revolutionary War veteran by the name of John Benjamin (new name Sarah Mary Benjamin). When John died in 1827, she was not eligible for a pension.[131] But in November 1837, at the age of eighty-one, she qualified and was awarded a pension as Osborn's widow. She received a pension of $88.00 a year and remained on the pension rolls for twenty-seven years.

Historic marker in Wayne County, PA

Source: Headstone of Mary.
Notice it is marked as "Soldier," not "camp follower."

Attempting to measure just how many Revolutionary War female soldiers served as camp followers but were not compensated can be difficult because the military evidence is lacking. Sarah's affidavit is rare. She divulged her story despite the embarrassment of her husband's polygamy and her abandonment. Her testimony indicates that other wives that followed their husbands also served as soldiers as well. As mentioned throughout this book, many women are not identifiable in the official military records. Why, you ask? Because they used male names, masqueraded as men in order to serve. Additionally, many women did not know how to read and write so therefore could not write down their ventures. Historians have to rely on journals from other soldiers, surgeon reports, pension requests, or newspaper articles of that time.

"I have not yet begun to fight." —**John Paul Jones**

CHAPTER 4
Spies

While the historiography of the American Revolutionary War is enormous, the unique and wide-ranging experiences of females are not commonly studied. The themes undertaken in this study include an overview of the various heroic deeds these women performed in the name of freedom. General George Washington realized he needed to know the British Army's strategic plans and their maneuvers, so he recognized that it was necessary to utilize spies (especially females) to defeat the British empire. In 1778, Washington appointed Major Benjamin Tallmadge as his chief of intelligence; he later formed and spearheaded a network of spies known as the Culper Spy Ring (1778-1780), also known as the Setauket Spy Ring, comprised of Long Island Patriots. The home base for this spy ring was in British-occupied New York City, Long Island, and Connecticut. What better place to have an elaborate spy ring than in the middle of enemy-occupied territory. Tallmadge first recruited Captain Nathan Hale of the 19th Regiment of the Continental Army. Unfortunately, Hale was executed by General William Howe as a spy in 1776.

The first unofficial spy ring started in Boston. They were known as the mechanics, and they were born out of the Sons of Liberty in the fall or winter of 1775. Paul Revere was one of their leaders. The "mechanics" (meaning skilled laborers and artisans, also known as the Liberty Boys) organized resistance to British authority and gathered intelligence.[132] Funny, they didn't teach this in grade school. They just regurgitated the fallacy that he was the longest writer to warn the colonists that the enemy was soon approaching. According to Revere, *"We frequently took turns, two and two, to watch the (British) soldiers by patrolling the streets all night."* The mechanics were not very good at spying. They met in the same place regularly (the Greene Dragon Tavern), and one of their leaders was Benjamin Church (some say he was a British spy). He was the

Source: Public Domain

A page from the Culper Ring's codebook, with noteworthy people and place names listed side by side with numerical representations.

Source: Library of Congress

Handwritten list of Culper Spy Ring cods, with 355 (lady) circled in red

first Surgeon General of the United States Army (July 1775 to October 1775). Did they not do background checks?

The Culper Spy Ring was better organized. These spies communicated in coded messages, letters written by invisible ink (invented by James Jay), and the recipients of the invisible-ink letters would use a liquid reagent to bring out the coded messages. George Washington referred to the concoction as the "sympathetic stain" and used the code word "medicine" in his future correspondence with James Jay.[133] The Culper espionage was funneled through the pastoral village of Setauket, and the base of the spiral operations was at Abraham Woodall's farm. Once Washington received reliable intelligence, he would share the information with French General Vice Admiral d'Estaing. Recorded vital members of the Culper spy ring were Abraham Woodall (farmer), Robert Townsend (a merchant), Austin Roe (tavern owner), other unnamed men, and two pivotal courageous spies named Agent 355 and Anna Smith (also known as Nancy).

AGENT 355

Many historians share several theories that Agent 355 might be Anna Smith Strong, Betty Floyd, or even Robert Townsend's common-law wife. No one knows who could possibly be Agent 355. Two hundred-plus years later, historians are still baffled as to who Agent 355 was. Was she a New York City socialite, servant, or an officer's wife? The Culper spy agents all reported to Abraham Woodhull, who went by the alias of Samuel Culper Sr. The number 355 is a cipher code that means "lady." In 1779, Woodhull wrote a letter to Tallmadge mentioning, "I intend to visit 727 (code for New York) before long and think by the assistance of a 355 (lady) of my acquaintance, shall be able to outsmart them all.'[134] This letter clearly demonstrates that the spy's identity must be hidden because she had the ability to be very close to the enemy in order to acquire and collect military intelligence that was vital to the Culper spy network.

It is speculated that Agent 355 is the one who played a significant part in exposing and passing critical information that revealed Major General Benedict Arnold's scheme to sell West Point to British General Sir Henry Clinton because the man was in debt and needed money. Intelligence was turned over to General Washington, informing him of the plot that led the Patriots to triumph over the British in the Revolutionary War. For five years, Agent 355 and the rest of the Culper spies reported the British Army's movement, number of troops, supply chains, intercepted communications, and reported the enemy's locations. Anna Smith Strong's role in the ring was to relay signals by hanging laundry on her clothesline in prearranged configurations. Anna would hang black clothing with handkerchiefs scattered throughout her wash line. This was a signal to Abraham Woodhull. Woodhull would count the white handkerchiefs, which indicated the six coves Caleb's boat was hidden in. Woodhull then contacted Caleb to pass along the secret messages from another spy ring member, Robert Townsend. It is also suspected that Agent 355 was responsible for the arrest of British intelligence leader Major John André and traitor Benedict Arnold. Oh, what did Benedict Arnold do, you ask? He planned to turn West Point over to the British, along with George Washington and his Continental Army. Benedict Arnold attempted to lure Washington to West Point, but he learned of this plan through intelligence provided by the Culper Spy Ring. Like a coward, Benedict Arnold fled back to England. He died in June 1801 from health complications and gout. Arnold's coconspirator, Major André, was in custody and hanged as a traitor in 1780.

General William Howe was sent to New York in August 1776 to negotiate peace with the American Rebels. However, these negotiations failed. General Howe invaded Long Island. Howe's troops outnumbered General Washington (twenty thousand American troops fought against thirty thousand (give or take) British troops, eight thousand Hessians, and thirty ships). Washington's back was to the East River. Washington had no choice but to withdraw from Long Island. However, his retreat allowed him to hold off the British from White Plains. Washington decided with his back to the river that he needed to defend Brooklyn Heights to rebuild his army. However, the Continental Congress ordered Washington to withdraw from New York. The British gained control of New Jersey in the winter of 1776 in the first Battle of Trenton (Anna Maria Lane was in this battle).

In 1780, Agent 355 was captured and imprisoned on His or Hers Majesty ships *(HMS),* New Jersey, located in New York's harbor, British prison ship that had sixty guns. There is no known documentation explaining how she was captured. Agent 355 was apprehended after Benedict Arnold defected to the Loyalists (around 1780). The conditions on board *HMS Jersey* were referred to by its inmates simply as "Hell."[135] Dozens of prisoners died each night from diseases, dysentery, smallpox, yellow fever, starvation, and torture. It is estimated that 11,000 prisoners died during the war on that specific prison ship.

Anna Smith Strong's husband, Selah Strong, was imprisoned in 1778 on the *HMS Jersey* for surreptitious correspondence with the enemy. It is believed Anna would bring her husband food and through her family connections was able to negotiate his release. During my research, I discovered many historians claimed that Agent 355 was pregnant while imprisoned in the *HMS New Jersey.* However, it would be a miracle if she went into full-term to give birth to a child in such severe conditions, nor would the child have survived after the birth. Intelligence correspondence from Agent 355 stopped in 1780 and it never resumed. It is assumed that she perished in the halls of the torture ship before 1783. Agent 355 could not possibly be Anna Smith Strong; she died of old age in 1812. Townsend's common-law wife Mary Margaret Banvard Townsend's housekeeper

Source: *wikipedia.org*

HMS Jersey

died in 1841. Neither woman claim to be Agent 355. You would think such an honorable position one would come forward and recount their heroism to encourage Patriotism for their country.

On March 21st, 2022, the Smithsonian history website published an article titled "The Myth of Agent 355: The Woman Spy Who Supposedly Helped Win the Revolutionary War." I won't name the author because I do not wish to embarrass him. The author claimed that Agent 355 was a myth. Simply made up to boost the morale of Patriotism. That seems to be the going theme. Male historians discredit females who were brave enough to take up arms against the enemy as being a fictitious story. With the evidence I provided, Agent 355 did indeed exist. The goal of being a successful spy is not to be detected, to basically be nonexistent, don't have a paper trail. The author of this article states she, Agent 355, did not exist because there wasn't a paper trail. How silly of him. Don't you just love when men exclude women from heroic deeds?

In *The Women of '76*, by Sally Smith Booth, published in 1976, the author mainly discusses well-known wives of Patriot leaders.[136] However, she did write about Agent 355 (Chapter 8) and stated that she bore a son to Robert Townsend. Sally Smith Booth provides no evidence to this theory. The author also writes about Grace and Rachel Martin (Chapter 9) but only contributes four sentences to both women. In *Glory, Passion, and Principle: The Story of Eight Remarkable Women at the Core of the American Revolution*, by Melissa Lukeman Bohrer, published in 2004, [137] in her chapter titled "Spy Games," the author speaks about Lydia Darragh, her family life, children, and husband. However, it read more of a romantic novel versus historical literature and mentioned she was a spy and delivered an important message to Washington. However, the author did not elaborate. So, the question is: Did you also come to the same conclusion, that Agent 355 died on the prison ship?

ANN SIMPSON DAVIS

On December 29, 1762, Anna was born to Irish immigrants in Buckingham Township, PA. Anna's father, William Simpson, was a soldier in the Revolutionary War and enlisted in 1775.[138] Her mother, Nancy (maiden name Hines), stayed home and tended to the farm. At sixteen, Anna served as a horse messenger under General Washington. Many historians state that she was handpicked personally by General Washington. However, there is no historical evidence or resources that prove this to be factual. Ann was an accomplished horsewoman and was a familiar sight to her Tory neighbors. Ann was the perfect candidate to slip unnoticed through the British ranks. Why, you ask? Well, she dressed as an old woman, which got her out of many tight spots. While researching Ann Simpson Davis, I found more information relaying the heroic deeds of her husband versus hers. Just a few sentences were contributed to Anne. Society has forgotten this brave soul. Wonder why that is? Is it because of her gender? Oh, please, let it not be that (sarcasm)!!

This young girl carried messages in sacks of grain and vegetables. She also smuggled bullets in her clothing. Ann rode back and forth from Washington to his Generals while in Eastern Pennsylvania. The Philadelphia Campaign was taking place from 1777-1778, with a total of seventeen battles that took place while Ann was a spy/messenger. Ann would frequent mills. This was a center for gossip and news, which everyone went to and which gave her added cover. Although she was never caught, it was rumored that she would memorize and swallow the messages before she was searched by the British or Tories.

General Washington employed women, girls, local, and foreign networks. He often did not know the identities of many of the people who spied for the Continental Army. However, Washington favored to meet his spies in person so he could judge their measure. And he judged Ann to be a notable Patriot. If not, he would not have used her to send messages. Using civilians as spies was an important military strategy. On several websites pertaining to Ann, I noticed they kept stating that she was a messenger from 1779 to 1780. However, that cannot be possible because battles in Pennsylvania were from 1777 to 1778. Sometime in December 1778, Washington moved the Continental Army into winter quarters around Middlebrook, New Jersey, thus ending her service as a spy/messenger.

GRAVES REGISTRATION CARD

Name .... Davis, Ann (Alias Davis, Ann Simpson) ....

Address .... - ....

Date of Death .... 6-5-1351 .... Place .... - ....

Cause .... - .... Date of Burial .... - ....

Date of Birth .... 12-29-1762 .... Place .... - Bucks County, Penna.

Name of Cemetery .... Davis Private .... Location .... Perry Twp. Franklin Co. ....

Lot No .... - .... Section No .... - .... Block No .... - .... Grave No. 145

Marker: Flat .... - .... Upright .... Monument .... None .... - ....

Next of Kin: .... - ....

(Name)   (Address)

SERVICE RECORD

War Served In: .... Revolutionary ....

Date Enlisted .... 1779 .... Date Discharged .... 1780 .... Serial No. .... -

Branch of Service .... Army .... Rank .... Messenger

Company, Outfit or Ship .... Messenger to Gen. Washington

Source: Ohio, Soldiers Grave Registration Cards, 1804-1958

This allowed him to maintain control of the Hudson River and protected critical Continental Army resources. In 1779, General Washington made strategic decisions that defeated the British offensive. So, therefore, the dates must be 1777 to 1778, not the latter. Pennsylvania played a critical role in the American Revolutionary War. Robert Morris (served as a member of the Pennsylvania legislature, the Second Continental Congress) once said, *"You will consider Philadelphia, from its centrical situation, the extent of its commerce, the number of its artificers, manufactures and other circumstances, to be to the United States what the heart is to the human body in circulating the blood."*

Even though her husband and Ann served in the American Revolutionary War, she applied for a pension under her husband's service and received a pension of a half yearly allowance of $40.00.[139]

In 1926, the Daughters of the American Revolution named a chapter after her. DAR claims that Ann received a letter of commendation from General Washington, thanking her for her service. Unfortunately, that letter cannot be located. Rumor has it that it was passed family member to family member and got lost over the years. After the war Ann married John Davis, on June 26, 1783, a veteran of the war. They lived in Maryland and moved to Dublin, Ohio, where they had several children (nine). They received a grant for services in the Revolutionary War and took up a land on the east side of the Scioto River, one

The following are the references to authorities for the above statements.

For the History of John Davis, the history is written in the history of Bucks County ,Pa, by William Watts Henry Davis of Doylestown Pa. who was a General in the Mexican War and held many positions in the the Army in the Civial War. Lived and died at Doylestown Pa. He was the president of the Bucks County Historical Society and wrote much about the Revolutionary War and the life of John Davis No.2.who became United States Senator from Pa. He was the son (John No.2)of John and Mary Ann Simpson Davis.

The muster rolls of Bucks County Pa ,also have the record and also also the Archives at Harrisburg Pa.

On the monument in the Davis Cemetery, located one mile South of Dublin Ohio,on Riverside Drive, there is engraved on the monuments, some history of John and Mary A nn Davis.

Mary Ann Simpson Davis served as a horse messenger under General Washington and carried messages to the other Generals.

Applicant affirms his adherence to the principles set forth in the Déclaration of Independence and his unqualified support of the Constitution of the United States of America, to the end that the inalienable rights of the citizen may be preserved and our ideal representative government perpetuated. See material deposited in his

Source: Application for membership, Ohio Society,

Sons of the American Revolution War, June 10th, 1954

DAVIS, ANN, (Franklin Co.)

Was a messenger and carried orders fr Gen Washington to the other commanders in the Revolutionary War in 1779 and 1780. Br 1763, Bucks Co, Pa. Mar John Davis. D June 6, 1851, Perry Twp. Bur Old Davis Cem 1 mi below Dublin, east side of Scioto River. She is buried under the same monument with her husband. MI: "Ann Davis died June 6, 1851, aged 88 years, 5 months, 8 days. Ann Davis was a messenger and carried orders from General Washington to the other commanders in 1779 and 1780." GM D. A. R. bronze marker, June 14, 1916. Ann Davis was a revolutionary heroine. Her maiden name was Ann Simpson and she was a cousin of the mother of General Grant. Columbus D. A. R. Chap, "Ann Simpson Davis" honors her name. Ref: Natl No 89528, Vol 90, D. A. R. Lin. Fur infor Columbus Chap.

Source: The official roster of the soldiers of the

American Revolution buried in the state of Ohio

mile south of Dublin, Franklin County, Ohio. Here is a fun fact about Anne: She was the cousin of General Grant's mother. Many of her descendants also showed Patriotism by being in every single American war since the American Revolution.

John died in 1832 and Anna died at the age of 87 in Dublin, Ohio, on June 6, 1851. Their war records are inscribed on either side of the monument located at the Davis Cemetery in Columbus, Ohio.

"All Washington could do was carry in his heart the gratitude he had for the sacrifices of his brave spies, which were no less meaningful for having been made in city streets and country back roads as on a battlefield."
—**Brian Kilmeade**

Source: Dublin Historical Society, the Dublin Branch of the Columbus Metropolitan Library, and the City of Dublin, the Dublin Memory Project Portrait of Ann Simpson Davis

LAODICEA "DICEY" LANGSTON

Dicey was born in 1760 or 1766; she was the daughter of Irish immigrant Solomon in the Ninety-Six District, South Carolina (you will learn more about that district later in this book). As many women who lived on farms were taught in the Colonial era, her father taught her how to shoot, hunt, and ride a horse. Dicey lived amongst the Loyalists in South Carolina. Her family supported the Patriot cause and everyone in her community knew this. Whenever Dicey heard any type of intelligence that would benefit the Continental Army, she would ride across the Enoree and Tyger rivers to her brother James' militia (her father was also in the militia). Eventually, the Tories became suspicious of her actions and threatened Solomon Sr., saying that they would hold him accountable for Dicey's actions. Solomon scolded her for putting the family in danger, so she stopped for a while. I wonder if he scolded her for not being so recluse in her spying missions. The benefit of sharing vital intelligence for the Patriot cause outweighed fear of her father. Historians disagree on the age at which she started to provide intelligence to the Patriots and local militia. Some say she started at fifteen, others say seventeen. In my opinion her age is not important, but her actions were.

The British Army invaded and occupied several American cities during the Revolutionary War. Some Americans fled, fearing that their lives were in danger; however, many colonists lived in their homes with the occupiers. Can you just imagine living day to day with the enemy? And in fear that at any moment they can kill you just because you disagreed with the king? This is exactly why America has the 4th Amendment. The British were very watchful of all Americans. There was a group of Loyalist soldiers in South Carolina called "The Bloody Scout." This group assassinated and took revenge on Patriots, which lasted several months in 1781. The leader of the Bloody Scouts was William Cunningham, also known as "Bloody Bill." This group committed massacres and murders throughout the state of South Carolina. The targets of these attacks were men and families who had been active in the Patriot cause. When Dicey overheard the Bloody Scouts planning to visit the "Elder Settlement" (a.k.a. Little Eden), twenty miles away, where her brother James' militia unit was located, she

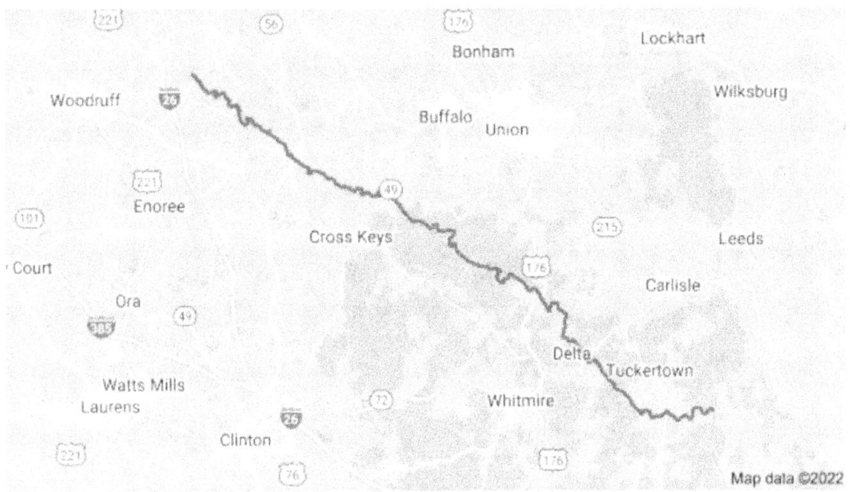

Source: Google Maps

Map of Tyger River, South Carolina

was determined to warn them. She leaped into action that night in the pouring rain. However, the bridges were washed out, so she swam across the Tyger River (807.9 square miles). Man, she must have really loved her brother and father. If it were my brother, perhaps I wouldn't do it. Perhaps I would. Who knows? Anyway, Dicey foiled the plans of the Bloody Scouts, because when they arrived at her brother's militia unit it was empty.

Dicey proved her bravery once again. One day she returned home from a town that had a heavy population of Whigs (supporters of the Patriots). The Whigs controlled the backcountry of South Carolina. The king's men failed to control South Carolina outside of the jurisdiction of the Ninety-Six. A company of Loyalists were waiting for her when she returned to town and demanded that she give them intelligence about the people she visited. This is where the story gets very interesting. Obviously, she refused—that was when the captain of the Loyalist militia put a gun to her chest, and still she did not disclose any information. Darcy put a handkerchief on her chest, offering a place for the weapon to fire. Luckily for her, another soldier threw up his hand to stop the captain from firing, saving her life. What a true Patriot she was, willing to die rather than give up information that would benefit the British. How many Americans in today's world would do the same?

In 1933 the Nathanael Greene chapter of the Daughters of the American Revolution dedicated a marker to Dicey for her bravery.

Dicey definitely has a fiery spirit. On another occurrence the Loyalists in the town wanted vengeance upon the intelligence they suspected Solomon's daughter relayed to the Whigs. A mob came to his house seeking to kill all the men in the family. Lucky for Solomon, his sons were away and only he and his teenage daughter were in the house. One of the Loyalists aimed a pistol at the old man, whereupon his daughter shrieked in anguish and jumped between the Loyalist and her father. The Loyalist took pity on this brave girl and her elderly father. One could only wonder if it was the same British soldier that saved her from the previous event. So, they departed. After all, only a very cruel individual would gun down an old man and his teenage daughter. And believe me, that did happen during the Revolutionary War, and all future wars. War is evil.

Dicey is noted in *Woman of the Revolution V.1,* by historian Elizabeth Ellet (published 1849), and in 2016 a children's book, *Rebel with a Cause: The Daring Adventure of Dicey Langston, Girl Spy of the American Revolution* (Encounter: *Narrative Nonfiction Picture Books*), by Jan Faber, was published telling the story of Dicey. Also, in 2008 Marnie Pehrson published *The Patriot wore Petticoats.*

Source: *Rebel with a Cause: The Daring Adventure of Dicey Langston, Girl Spy of the American Revolution* (Encounter: *Narrative Nonfiction Picture Books*) by

Perhson regurgitated what Elizabeth wrote in 1849. After 2008, Dicey's patriotism to the American cause was so great, it earned her the pseudonym "Daring Dicey." She is also noted in several children's books. South Carolina Revolutionary-era biographies published an online pamphlet titled *South Carolina Biography Revolutionary Women.* Laodicea "Dicey" Langston Springfield states that Dicey married Thomas Springfield at the age of sixteen.

Even though there are few books published about this heroin after the American Revolutionary War, society as a whole still doesn't know her name. Distinguished historians failed to include her when writing about the history of South Carolina and her bravery. Dicey died on May 23rd, 1837. Below is her obituary:

Died on Tuesday, the 23rd, Mrs. Laodicea Springfield, aged 71 years, wife of Thomas Springfield. The deceased was the daughter of Solomon Langston of Revolutionary memory, whose family perhaps suffered more from the ruthless ravages of the Tories and Indians than almost any other, and the subject of this remark took an active part in the struggle and performed many daring deeds on behalf of her suffering country and friends. She was the mother of 22 children and has left about 140 grand and great grandchildren. She was a kind and affectionate wife, mother, and neighbor, and has left a large circle of acquaintances to deplore her loss.

There is a petition to create a life-size statue of Dicey. There is a Go Fund Me for the statue project. They are asking 450K but to this date they only have 5K. If you wish to donate, you can find it under "Dicey Langston statue project." I hope Dicey's heroinism inspired you and also made you realize that many women are written out of history books mainly because of their gender and social status.

HANNAH MILLIKAN BLAIR

Hannah was born on January 14th, 1756, in Pennsylvania. Her father was William Millikan Sr. (1720-1804), who assisted the Patriots. Sadly, Hannah's mother died when she was just three years old (Martha Jane White, 1720-1759). She was a Quaker and mother of thirteen live births (births between 1776-1794). At the age of nineteen, Hannah married her first husband, Hans Enos (1750–1834). Blair (goes by Enos) was another Quaker on May 10, 1775, in Guilford, North Carolina. I cannot locate the name of her first husband. She provided food and medicine and mended their uniforms; it is speculated that she also delivered messages for them. These soldiers were hidden in the woods from Tory raiders. During the war, Continental soldiers and Patriot militias often disappeared into the woods to hide from Loyalist raiders. Hannah is credited with saving the lives of two men when she hid them in a corn crib and continued shucking corn while the Tories searched. Another famous recorded account is when the infamous Loyalist leader Colonel David Fanning searched for Patriots near Hannah's home. Hearing this, Hannah, hid a few Patriots in a feathered bed by ripping the corner open and pushed the Patriot inside. She threw the covers back so Colonel Fanning could see clearly under the bed. Hannah sat down and began mending a torn section of the sheets, saying, *"Thee may search as thee pleases."*

After a skirmish at Dixon's Mill in North Carolina 1779, she learned that several soldiers were hiding in the countryside and took provisions to them. As she was returning, she was taken by Tories, who demanded to know where the men were hiding. Hannah insisted that she had only taken food to a sick neighbor ten miles away. The British released her. Tories, however, did not believe her and suspected her as a spy, and in 1782 they burned down the Blairs' house and barn, and the family was forced to watch.[140] That is correct, the Tories and Patriots burned their enemies' houses. Hannah was left with nothing but the clothes on her back. Hannah being involved in any war directly conflicts with the Quaker religious beliefs. The Quakers first came to America in the 1650s with a strong headquarters in Pennsylvania. Around 1776, after the Declaration of Independence, the Quaker religion declared neutrality between the British and the

The first of his name to arrive in North Carolina. Millikan came from Chester County. Pa.. in 1758. one of a group of Quakers. During the Revolutionary War he and his family were intensely patriotic. espousing the American cause. In the course of events during the war. his home and barns were burned by David Fanning. the infamous Tory.

After the war, both William. and his daughter, Hannah Blair. were pensioned by the government for their heroic acts of patriotism. William Millikan became the first registrar of deeds of Randolph County. a justice of the peace. a surveyor, and holder of many other important offices.

Source: The High Point Enterprise (High Point, North Carolina), August 7, 1976

Rebels. Her father, William, also participated in helping the Patriots; he too furnished goods to the Americans.[141] Judith Mower Goodman, *History of the Blair Family* (Blair genealogy file, Quaker Collection, Guilford College, Greensboro), published in 1969, is a good reference to the family history of the Blairs. It seems that her bravery is recorded through family legend and a few biographies published in the 1800s. How many Americans in today's society would do the same if there was ever another war on our soil? Would you? I combed through the online newspaper archives and discovered one article speaking about a pension. At left is an image.

Some historians claim that Hannah Blair's story of bravery is fantastical and painted a picture of a woman who came to the aid of Patriot militia and Continental soldiers hiding in the woods. Why is it so hard to believe that a woman is capable of such bravery and compassion? Why does society still view women as second-class citizens? So how were these deeds recorded? How did the government become aware of Hannah's deeds versus her father's? The only pension I can locate in the National Archives was for her father, William. And that pension did not mention his daughter Hannah's heroic deeds. After the war was awarded a pension by the government for their heroic acts of Patriotism, on November 2, 1784, she and her father acquired 400 acres on Back Creek.

Source: *Findagrave.com,* headstone of Hannah Blair

At the age of 83 Hannah married her second husband in 1840, a gentleman named Solomon Fraser (1816-1904). Now, I am no mathematician, but that seems to be a sixty-year difference. Hannah was born in 1756 and her second husband born in 1816. Good for her! Still got it! Hannah had a baby every year during the American Revolution with her first husband. This woman managed to provide soldiers with food, shelter, and supplies, and evaded capture. What she was doing was in line with her Quaker religious beliefs. Oh, what is a Quaker? It is The Society of Friends, better known as Quakers, who are taught to be pacifists and had (or still have) anti-authority beliefs.

Hanna died in 1852 at the tender age of 95 in North Carolina. She is buried next to her first husband, Enos, in Springfield Friends Meeting House Cemetery High Point, Guilford County, North Carolina.[142]

LYDIA BARRINGTON DARRAGH

Lydia Barrington Darragh, originally from Dublin, Ireland, was a Quaker, mother of five, and married to Lieutenant William Darragh. However, the Quaker religion did not stop Lydia's oldest son, Charles, from serving in the Continental Army (2nd Pennsylvania Regiment). In 1777, British General William Howe took control and occupied Philadelphia. Nearly one-third of Philadelphia's population evacuated the city and most of those remaining were Loyalists. In the Fall of that year, General George Washington led an unsuccessful attempt to retake Philadelphia from the British. He retreated to Whitemarsh. Lydia and her family remained in their home, assuming that they were safe because of their religious convictions.

However, British officers, along with Lydia's cousin Lieutenant Barrington, who decided to join the British Army, arrived at Lydia's house demanding to utilize their large upstairs room for military meetings. The Darragh family had no place to go, so they begged the British to remain in their own house. The British agreed. On the night of December 2, 1777, Howe held a secret conference. Lydia always listened in on the conversations and passed along the intelligence. Lydia would place her covert notes into her coat and pass them onto the Patriot troops stationed outside of Philadelphia at Valley Forge, the Continental Army's winter encampment. Sometimes she sewed the messages into button covers or hid them in needlebooks. Spying on the British occupiers ran in the family. Historian Debra Michals (Ph.D.) published a biography on Lydia in the National Woman's History Museum. Dr. Michals claims that Lydia's fourteen-year-old son, John, smuggled her coded notes about British activities she overheard in the tavern across the street to her eldest son, Charles, a Patriot soldier.[143] However, according to The American Battlefield Trust, Lydia obtained the secret messages herself, not her son, and delivered them to her older son Charles. The point is her eldest son received the covert messages his mother intended for him to have.

In December 1777, she learned that the British planned on attacking Washington, known as the Battle of White Marsh (1777). On December 2, 1777, Lydia set off to warn General Washington. She came up with a plan and told the British troops that she needed flour and wished to visit her other children and had to leave the city and requested an exit pass.[144] On her way to warn the general of the pending attack, she stopped by the Rising Sun Tavern, a covert Patriot message center. There she encountered Colonel Elias Boudinot (who became a congressman for NJ after the war). Elias Boudinot wrote in his journal a detailed account of his role in passing on intelligence to General Washington about a possible British attack that he received on the night of December 3, 1777. Here is what he wrote:

In the Autumn of 1777, the American Army lay some time at White Marsh. I was then Commissary Gen. of Prisoners and managed the Intelligence of the Army. I was reconnoitering along the Lines near the City of Philadelphia. I dined at a small Post at the rising Sun about three miles from the City. After Dinner a little poor looking insignificant Old Woman came in & solicited leave to go into the Country to buy some flour— While we were asking some Questions, she walked up to me and put into my hands a dirty old needlebook, with various small pockets in it. surprised at this, I told her to return, she should have an answer—On opening the needlebook, I could not find anything till I got to the last Pocket, where I found a piece of Paper rolled up into the form of a Pipe Shank. On unrolling it I found information that Gen. Howe was coming out the next morning with 5000 Men, 13 pieces of cannon, Baggage Wagons, and 11 Boats on Wagons Wheels. On comparing this with other information I found it true, and immediately rode Post to head Quarters. According to my usual Custom & agreeable to orders rec from Gen. W. I first related to him the naked facts without comment or Opinion—He rec. it with much thoughtfulness, I then gave him my opinion, that Gen. Howe's design was to Cross the Delaware under pretense of going for New York. Then in the Night to recross the Delaware above Bristol & come suddenly on Our Rear, when we were totally unguarded and cut off all our Baggage, if not the whole Army. He heard me without a single observation, being deep in thought. I repeated my observations. He still was silent—supposing myself unattended to I earnestly repeated my Opinion, with urging him to order a few redoubts thrown up in our rear, as it was growing late. The Gen. Answered me, Mr. Boudinot the Enemy have no business in our rear. The Boats are designed to deceive us. Tomorrow morning by day light you will find them coming down such a bye Road on our left. Then calling an Aid du Camp ordered a line thrown up along our whole front at the foot of the Hill. As I was quartered on that very Bye Road with 6 or 8 other Officers, a Mile in front of our Army, and no Pickett advanced of us. This opinion made a deep Impression upon me Tho' I thot the General under a manifest mistake. I returned to my Quarters first obtaining a Pickett to be put on that road in Advance. [145]

So, there is the firsthand evidence that Lydia passed the intelligence on versus her son. It could be that she used her son at some point. However, this firsthand account states that Lydia was the one who saved the day. Washington's troops were ready and waiting in the cold white snow in the White Marsh Township, located in Pennsylvania. After several days of skirmish, Howe was forced to return to Philadelphia. This battle was one of the last significant engagements of 1777. While retreating to Philadelphia, Howe knew someone leaked the information and launched an investigation as to who revealed the attack to Washington. Lydia was questioned by British officers. She denied even knowing a meeting took place; she claimed all the family members in the house were asleep. Being a Quaker, they believed her and had no reason to suspect her spying merely because of her religious convictions.

Later in life, Lydia told her spy stories to her daughter Ann. Ann recounts a story her mother told her in a published biography in the *American Quarterly Review* (1827); she took off her shoes and put her ear to the conclave's keyhole. She overheard an order read for all the British troops to march out late in the evening of the fourth and attack general Washington's army.[146] Ann published a biography of her mother's veracity and was questioned by many scholars. In *Glory, Passion, and Principle: The Story of Eight Remarkable Women at the*

Core of the American Revolution, by Melissa Lukeman Bohrer, published in 2004,[147] in her chapter titled "Spy Games," the author speaks about Lydia Darragh, her family life, children, and husband. However, it read more of a romantic novel versus historical literature and mentioned she was a spy and delivered an important message to Washington, but the author did not elaborate. In 1909, Colonel Elias Boudinot corroborated Lydia Darragh's courageous spy efforts in his published memoirs. As he described the event in his memoirs of the war, Boudinot's account suggests that Darragh hid a note in an old cloth needlebook and passed the information to him that way.[148] Lydia Barrington Darragh died on December 28, 1790, in Philadelphia County, Pennsylvania. Below is her obituary:

On Tuefday evening laft died Mrs. Lydia Darragh, and on Thurfday her remains were interred in the Friends burial ground, attended by a numerous concourfe of forrowful citizens. She had experienced fome fhare of thofe ills attendant on humanity, and applied herfelf to a profeffion, in which the female part of fociety experienced her fkill, tendernefs and affiduity—To all fhe extended her fympathy. The poor and unfortunate will long, and the wealthy do now lament the lofs of it. She found the rewards of decent competency, of univerfal refpect, and the " bleffing of many ready to perifh." Let her example enliven the hope of the induftrious, and give ftrength to the virtuous—trufting, as fhe always did in her fevereft afflictions, that a good Providence will, in due time, blefs the labors of the compaffionate and tender-hearted.

Source: *Findagrave.com*, Memorial ID: 28814348

"There will never be a new world order until women are a part of it."
—Alice Paul

ANN NANCY HART

Ann Nancy Hart (maiden name Morgan) was a frontierswoman in North Carolina in 1735. Ann was a Patriot who was very vocal about the need for freedom from England and proud to protect America's liberty. She is described as having red hair, stood six feet tall, blue eyes (crossed), and was muscular. Another family member was also as Patriotic as Anne. She was cousin to General Daniel Morgan (1735-1802), who was in the battle of Cowpens in South Carolina 1781 and defeated the British. Many historians claim that the stories of Ann are "unsupported and made-up fairy tales." In 1901 a newspaper article written by R. J. Massey stated that Nancy Hart is a story of fiction and that it was no such person in real life, and that it was just a pretty story that was written by a clever writer. After that article was posted, many newspapers around the U.S. regurgitated what R. J. Massey stated in his original article. Well, my friend, I am here to set the record straight.

Ann was married in 1771 to Captain Benjamin Hart (1730-1799); she had six sons and two daughters. Later in life Ann moved to Georgia and was a notorious female rebel and spy. The Cherokee called her Wahatche, which means "war woman," and was illiterate. She served as a spy to the Georgia Whigs, under Colonel Elijah Clarke.[149] Ann disguised herself as a crazy man wandering through British camps pretending to be feeble-minded. It is alleged that Ann and her husband and sons were present at the Battle of Kettle Creek, Georgia (1779), where the Georgia militia and four hundred Patriot forces defeated six hundred British Loyalists under Colonel John Boyd. While researching archived newspapers from the Atlantic constitution from 1779 to the present, there is no indication that Ann, Benjamin, and her sons were on the battlefield. Now, that doesn't mean they were not there. This only means there is no recorded evidence. There were a total of forty-two battles and skirmishes fought during the Revolutionary War in Georgia. Locally the battle of Kettle Creek is well publicized. However, outside of Georgia it seems to be an unimportant Revolutionary War engagement between British and American forces. The British regularly harassed Patriot women while their husbands were away at war.

On one occasion, Hart's daughter noticed a British soldier spying through a hole in the wall. Hart threw a boiling ladle through the hole, scalding the spy. She and one of her daughters then tied him up and turned him over to the Patriots. Hart's most famous act involved five or six British soldiers, who killed her last turkey and demanded that she prepare it for them. In 1825, *The Savannah Republican* published this well-known story from the *Milledgeville Recorder,* describing the story as incontrovertible facts.[150] The story says Hart developed a plan to get the soldiers drunk on corn whiskey (moonshine). While the soldiers ate and drank, Hart began sneaking their guns out through a hole in the wall. One of the drunken soul British soldiers took notice of what Nancy was doing. She immediately drew their weapon and threatened to shoot them. One soldier boldly rushed at her. She killed him instantly and injured another. The rest surrendered.

Hart instructed her daughter to go down to the spring and blow the conch shell (large seashell), alerting neighbors of the British presence. Her husband returned that very night. He and some neighbors hung the soldiers from a nearby tree in Elberton, Georgia. In 1912, Railroad workers unearthed six bodies buried near the Hart home, evidence of the British soldiers hanged, giving credence to the Hart legend.[151] POW!! Factual evidence, my friend.

SKELETONS OF SIX TORIES HANGED NEAR ELBERTON, FOUND

Athens, Ga., December 22.—(Special.) Skeletons of the six Tories captured at her dinner table and afterwards hanged to trees near her home by Nancy Hart more than a century and a half ago, were unearthed last week by a squad of hands at work grading the Elberton and Eastern railroad. They were buried about three feet under the ground in what is known as the Heard field, near the mouth of Wahatchie creek, some half a mile from where it empties into Broad river. The bones are all there, in a splendid state of preservation, but have become disjointed. The skulls, in fact, all the bones of the heads and under jaws, are especially well preserved and the teeth are perfect.

The place where the skeletons were unearthed, together with the fact that they were so close together, near the surface, with no sign or trace of anything like a coffin anywhere around, makes the evidence convincing that these are the bones of the Tories captured by the revolutionary heroine who lives in history as the crossest-eyed and ugliest, as well as the bravest and most loyal woman of the period.

The house that Nancy Hart lived in was located on Wahatchie creek near a spring some half to three-fourths of a mile from where the skeletons were found. The place is now owned by the local chapter of the Daughters of the American Revolution. Jim Bradford, of the county, who recently died at the advanced age of about 90 years, remembered about his father and the older people of his boyhood days telling all about the house that Nancy lived in, and pointed out the place where the Tories were hanged, which is, as near as can be now located, just where the railroad laborers unearthed the skeletons.

This place is about thirteen miles from Elberton.

Source: *The Atlantic Constitution Newspaper,* December 23, 1912

Georgia Governor (served from 1790-1859) George Rockingham Gilmer also served several terms in the U.S. House of Representatives (not a good guy, wrote laws to take the land of Indigenous tribes), wrote a book titled *Georgians* in 1855, and devoted an entire chapter to Ann. In 1930 Congress recognized Nancy Hart and tributed a highway in Georgia to honor her. Congress acknowledges her as an American pioneer and her heroic service in the cause of freedom during the Revolutionary War.

Nancy Hart died in 1823 and was buried in the Hart Family Cemetery near Frog Island in Kentucky. Till her last breath, Nancy still was a zealous supporter of the Patriotic cause.

Many historians suggest that Nancy Hart is nothing but a creation of a romantic story during the Revolutionary War. However, cooperating evidence debunks that myth. Why is it difficult for a dominant-male society to accept that a female is capable of doing such patriotic heroic deeds?

Not all women are fragile; many are Amazonians, just like Ann Nancy Hart. Occasionally, it is challenging to separate fact from the myth, as her admirers embellished the particulars of her patriotic achievements to the point where they took on Amazonian proportions. In a way Nancy Hart was, by definition, an Amazonian.

Source: DAR records

Ann Nancy Morgan Heart

Source: *Findagrave.com,*
MEMORIAL ID 16616031

Source: *Findagrave.com,* MEMORIAL ID 16616031

Nancy Heart's headstone

SARAH "SALLY" TOWNSEND

Sally was born in 1761, Oyster Bay, New York. It is speculated that Sally was a member of the Culper Spy Ring and that she passed information to her brother Robert Townsend, who we now know is a prominent member of the spy ring. Samuel Townsend's home (Sarah's father) was occupied by British Lieutenant Colonel John Simcoe, commander of the Queen's Rangers. The Townsend family pretended to be British Loyalists. The reason behind this is when Britain took over New York, only families that pledged allegiance to the king were able to remain in their homes. So they lied and said, yeah, sure, we love the king. Some say that Sally was the actual spy who assisted in discovering Benedict Arnold's attempt to turn over George Washington's army at West Point to the British. Well, if you remember when I discussed Agent 355, I put that to rest. However, some say that Sarah overheard British Officer John Graves Simcoe speaking to Major John André about their plans to take West Point using leaked intelligence from turncoat Benedict Arnold. However, there is no tangible evidence supporting that claim, just hearsay.

On September 23rd, 1780, three West Chester militiamen were on patrol near Tarrytown. A man who identified himself as John Anderson carried in his boot the plans for West Point and a safe-conduct message signed by General Benedict Arnold, the turncoat. In reality, Anderson was Major André. The leader of the Culper ring signed by General George Washington was Sally's brother Robert. His code name was Culper Jr. I wonder who Sr. was? According to historian Dorothy Horton McGee, Sally wrote in her journal that she had seen Andre go to a cupboard in their house (called the Raynham Hall), pick up a hidden message addressed to John Anderson, and had overheard him whispering about West Point to another British officer. However, the note does not exist. It's a story. There's no tangible evidence. Three Westchester militiamen (Patriot side), Van Wart, John Paulding, and David Williams, who were on sentry duty, stopped a man one night riding on horseback near Tarrytown. The man wore a Continental Army coat over his British uniform and carried a pass signed by General Benedict Arnold. The rider stated he was John Anderson and tried to bribe his way out of the situation. However, the militiamen ordered the rider to strip, including his boots.

When the rider took off his boots, that's when the note dropped out. So technically, these three men, whose story was regurgitated through family members, are the true heroes that stopped Benedict Arnold. Not Agent 355 or Sally Townsend. Or is the tale factual versus fiction? Again, no tangible evidence other than a great-great-granddaughter reciting the story and a newspaper published the same story in 1980. So, the story of when Benedict Arnold was caught is half history and half legend. The main point is that General Washington was warned in time, and the Continental Army was out of danger. Agent 355, Sally Townsend, and these three militiamen were responsible for West Point's safety. Sally and her family remained in New York after the war. The Townsend house is now a historical landmark. Sally died in December 1842; she never married and lived with her older brother Robert Townsend.

These examples of female spies in this book prove that many women (not all) possess the wisdom, strength, and courage to fight against a tyrannical government. Although one or two of the written examples show that the women intercepted intelligence once or twice, the domino effect of the intelligence they handed over to the Patriots impacted the outcome of this war. Women have fought in wars as soldiers and spies since the beginning of time, and they should not be excluded from history because some view their gender as a symbol of shame. Female spies from the Revolutionary War and today are potent symbols considered by many as a threat to masculinity. Women do not deserve to be omitted from history because various historians may have unconsciously biased toward females. Civilized societies have become militarized, which needs muscle, physical power, and strength, thus leaving females out of historical expansions because they still need to meet the status quo. If it were not for Washington's nameless spies, both men and women, the independent United States of America would have only been a dream, not a reality.

"Give me liberty or give me death!"
—Patrick Henry

CHAPTER 5
Heroines

According to Merriam-Webster's dictionary, a heroine is a woman admired and emulated for her achievements and qualities. A mythical individual legendary woman often of divine descent has excellent strength or ability.[152] The definition of a hero (male) is a person admired for great or brave acts or fine qualities, a warrior who shows great courage, a mythical individual. The one key difference in both definitions is that the male description states a hero is a warrior but not the female definition. These two definitions attempt to challenge the nature of hero and heroine are woefully inadequate. The definitions emphasize physical strength, mythology and are absent in clarifying intellect as a characteristic. The women in this chapter are not mythical and represent heroism and are barely mentioned in history books. These are not masculine females; their heroic deeds involve courageous selfless actions who helped those in need, while under dangerous circumstances. These women risked their lives in doing so. The examples of these heroines will teach generations to come in defining one's limits and perhaps become an inspiration. The Greek philosopher Aristotle defines courage in his Nicomachean Ethics (written B.C. 350) as consisting of confidence in the face of fear, that courageous persons feared only things that are worthy of fear and is a marker of moral excellence. I often wondered how many women in the 21st century have the moral courage and the commitment to stand up and act on their ethical beliefs. Acting on ethical values is to help others during complex dilemmas. These dilemmas would violate an individual's human rights. How many of us would stand up and say something versus just complain on social media?

EMILY GEIGER

Emily was born around 1765, in South Carolina. Her father, John Geiger (1748-1817), was in the local militia in Colonel Philemon Waters' Regiment (until he became disabled). The family immigrated from Switzerland. Emily's mother was Ann Muff (1742-1831). Emily married her first husband, Benjamin Drury Culpepper, in 1789. She had a total of six children with him. The South Carolina ETV Commission website states that Emily decided to volunteer and assisted General Nathaniel Greene in June of 1781.[153] After General Greene abandoned the siege to take control of the British Ninety-Six (June 1781), he retreated across the Saluda River in South Carolina and was pursued by Lorde George Augustus Francis Rawdon.[154] Greene was anxious to send dispatches to General Thomas Sumter, commander of the South Carolina militia. However, the countryside was infested with Tories. In 1780, Major Patrick Ferguson was appointed Inspector of Militia Corps to raise and organize Loyalists from the Tory population in the Carolina backcountry, to protect the left flank of Cornwall's main body, located in Charlotte, NC. Ferguson was also known to be very cruel to colonials who supported the Patriot cause. General Greene asked the men in his camp who would volunteer to dispatch these important messages through seventy miles of difficult terrain. No one volunteered; the soldiers were fearful of the number of Tories that were in the area and thought it was a suicide mission. So, General Greene sent out word to the surrounding areas asking for help from civilians. Word got to Emily (a teenager, age sixteen, some historians say she was eighteen) and she immediately got on her horse to seek out General Greene's camp. Emily and her family were strong supporters of the Patriot cause.

In 1890, the *Boston Weekly Globe* published an article titled "What One Girl Did." The article states that Emily was at Greene's camp, walked into his tent, and volunteered to dispatch the message because his soldiers feared being captured by the Tories. I wonder if General Greene thought that this teenage girl had more courage than his men to deliver his dispatches. I'm pretty sure he was shocked that a teenage girl was willing to risk her life for the Patriot cause versus his seasoned soldiers. It seemed like a logical solution to his problem; besides, Emily knew the backcountry and she explained that she delivered messages for other Patriots in the

EMILY GEIGER AND GREENE'S MESSAGE.
Source: The Library Company of Philadelphia
Geiger, Emily (1762 or 1763), Emily Geiger and Greeneee's message

past. General Greene's message explained strategies on how to conduct raids and skirmishes against British forces. Emily knew the dangers, and also knew that the Tories were spreading the word throughout the South that a female courier was spying for the Continental Army. If she was caught with the message she would be hung as a spy and her body would be displayed as an example to other Patriots who wished to help defeat the British. Unbeknownst to Emily, a Tory spy was in General Greene's camp and overheard other troops speaking about a girl delivering the message. The spy saw her leave camp and followed her.

General Greene was on the mission to stop the British Southern Strategy from succeeding. Unbeknownst to the Continental Army in 1779, British General Sir Henry Clinton had to give up two thousand troops for Canada's battle, which stretched his Army ultra-thin. By the time Clinton was to partake in the southern strategy, his two thousand troops were never replaced, and he was ordered to send more reinforcements to Jamaica. He had no choice other than to abandon his push to the South and withdraw from Newport. The British did not have a mighty force to conquer the South. It would take Emily one hundred miles (should have been

Source: *Ancestry.com*
Portrait of Emily Geiger

seventy, but she took the backcountry) to deliver the dispatch to Sumter. Unsuspecting, Emily was not aware her every move was being reported by a Tory spy. She continued her journey until she was forced to stop for the night and stayed with strangers, who were secretly Tories. The spy reported her activities to a man named Lowry, who in turn sent soldiers to apprehend Emily. Instead of immediately taking Emily into custody, these soldiers decided to rest for a few hours. Emily figured out what was happening, and while the Tories and soldiers slept she slipped out the window, saddled her horse, and rode off into the night. Three miles away from completing her mission (three miles from General Sumter's camp) she stumbled across three British soldiers. Man, talk about bad luck. The soldiers took Emily captive. They took her to Fort Granby, which was a mile away. The male soldiers were reluctant to search Emily due to her sex. However, a Tory female was requested to conduct the search. While waiting to be searched by the Tory female, Emily panicked; she memorized the message and swallowed it before she was searched. This was her only hope in escaping punishment or death if she was caught with the dispatch. She was then taken to be questioned by Lord Rawdon, who later released her when no communication was found on her person. Emily located General Sumter and delivered the message. General Sumter joined Greene at the Battle of Eutaw Springs in 1781. This was one of the battles Sally St. Clair fought in before her death. Some historians claim that Emily was a career spy for the Continental Army. However, there is no evidence to supporting that claim. Perhaps she was a spy; a good spy would never be on record.

Emily remarried to a John Threewits and they had one daughter together. Her first husband, John Geiger, died in 1829. Guess that relationship did not work out.

Remember the historian Elizabeth Ellet that I wrote about when discussing Laodicea "Dicey" Langston? Well, she also discovered journals written about Emily's heroic deeds in the university's archives. The author states there is no reason to doubt its authenticity. In 1848 Ellet published a book titled *Women of the American Revolution, Vol. II*, recounting Emily's brave act. She was simply a teenage girl who did her patriotic duty and delivered a message for General Greene. In 1930, without giving any reasonable explanation Alexander S. Salley Jr., Secretary of the South Carolina Historical Commission, charged that the Emily Geiger story was probably fiction. He declared it fiction because he found no correspondence between the two generals speaking of Emily. The generals had hundreds of couriers to deliver their messages. In a time of war, it's not reasonable to jot down who is your courier. You do not want those names to get into the wrong hands. In my humble opinion it's just another man trying to disgrace a woman who stepped up when men did not. In 1931 a relative of Emily signed a sworn affidavit to Honorable T. Roots Davis, senator of South Carolina, which stated the following:

> *My great-grandmother was the youngest daughter of John Conrad Geiger and was born and reared about three miles below Granby, Lexington county, on what is known as the old Charleston road. I heard her on many occasions tell as a fact that Emily Geiger, her first cousin, delivered a message from Gen. Greene to Gen. Sumter, during the Revolutionary war, and that she was captured and searched by the Tories, and finding*

> *no incriminating evidence about her person, in view of the fact that she had swallowed the note, released her; that after her release she spent the night at my said great grandmother's home, who was at that time a girl of ten or twelve years of age; that ray said great grandmother told me that Emily Geiger, on the night spent at her home, related in detail the circumstances of her ride, arrest and release.*[155]

Emily appeared in the *Bangor Daily Whig and Courier* newspaper, published in 1849 by T. S. Arthur, titled "Emily Geiger, the Fair Courier." The article recounts Emily's brave actions in delivering the message to Sumter. However, he attempted to romanticize Emily, stating that she was a beautiful eighteen-year-old woman and Greene could not resist her request, when in fact she was a sixteen-year-old child. In 1974, the Daughters of the American Revolution, the Emily Geiger Chapter, dedicated a memorial marker at Emily's gravesite. Elizabeth Ellet's effort to immortalize the name of Emily Geiger seems to have succeeded. Once Ellet's book was published, Emily's story spread throughout the South Carolinas like wildfire. Many newspapers republished the author's story of a female Patriot.

Emily died in 1825 (age sixty); her grave marker was moved to the Geiger Cemetery in 1958.

"Life doesn't get easier; you just get stronger."
—Emily Geiger

ELIZABETH BURGIN

Elizabeth was resided in New York City; she had three children and became widowed around 1778. Historians are unsure as to how her husband died. Linda Kuester from North Manchester Historical Society claims that Elizabeth was a Quaker but provides no evidence to this claim. Elizabeth began bringing food to Continental soldiers being held as captives on British prison ships located in New York's harbor. From 1776 to 1783, the British imprisoned thousands of Patriots on *HMS Jersey* (Agent 355 was also a prisoner on this ship) in New York. In 1779, she was approached by George Washington to help prisoners of war escape the prison ships. American Patriot prisoners preferred death at its worst rather than disloyalty to their country. These Patriots could have betrayed the cause of liberty and America's independence in exchange for their lives, but they did not. That, my friend, is the definition of patriotism. To be granted freedom, the British prisoners had to sign a document of allegiance to the Crown, giving them a full pardon, and enlist in His Majesty's army or navy. So, in other words, be a traitor to your countrymen. Unfortunately, one of Burgin's coconspirators, George Higday, was arrested for espionage. Higday assisted Elizabeth with crossing the escaped Patriots from the prison ship across the river to freedom.

She found herself in New Jersey with her three children at the time. She was a refugee from New York City with no property or livelihood; in the letter she requested assistance. She had good handwriting. However, the spelling and grammar were terrible. Remember, in the Colonial era, many women were not allowed to learn how to read and write. On November 19th, 1779, Elizabeth wrote a letter to James Caldwell (a Presbyterian minister who played a prominent part in the American Revolution). In July 1779, British Major General James Pattison suspected Elizabeth of helping American prisoners escape from a prison ship (name unknown). Those prisoners were George Higday, who served as a spy courier, and Major Leonard Van Buren's escape from captivity in New York.

Van Buren wrote a letter to Burgin from Albany on November 26, 1779. It reads:

The news of your escape reached me shortly after you had affected it, I immediately after went down to West-point in search of you where I was informed that you was gone to Philadelphia, it Surprised me much that you did not come up to this place according to your provision, nothing will give me more pleasure than to See you at my Father's House where you may Live, till you can with pleasure and Safety return to your place of abode, by the Bearer hereof Mr. John Blair I send you five Hundred Dollars which I beg you to accept of If you should be in want of any more please to call on Sd person and he will let you have what you want or if you wish to purchase and he has it he will give you Credit till you can make returns, Enclosed I send you a Certificate of the kind treatment prisoners rec'd from your hands, which I thought might be of Service to you.

Burgin also wrote that the captured American had *"carried out two hundred American prisoners for me."* The meaning of this sentence is not clear, but it's the only detail that Burgin wrote about what she'd been doing.[156] General Washington learned of George's situation. Washington wrote to Benjamin Tallmadge, who was in the process of creating the Culper Spy Ring, and informed him that Higday might be helpful. Unfortunately, just after receiving the general's update, Tallmadge's camp was attacked by the British, who knew that he was involved with Patriot espionage. In his saddle was the letter from Washington, which mentioned George Higday by name (along with money and information for the rest of the spy ring). The British searched for Higday, and he was finally arrested in his home. Higday became a turncoat and wrote a confession of the prison escape and gave Elizabeth up as a spy. Elizabeth got word and was forced into hiding. Even though Higday gave Elizabeth's name as a spy, there's absolutely no evidence that suggests that she was one. What she did was rescue hundreds of Continental Army officers and privates from a prison ship.

Elizabeth and her children hid for two weeks while British guards watched her house, and a reward of £200 was offered for her capture. Thankfully, some friends aided her travels to Long Island, where they went into hiding for another five weeks. She left her children in hiding to travel to Connecticut on a whaleboat, from there to Philadelphia, then New Jersey. It is unknown how she arranged for her children to be sent to her, but they were. That's when she wrote her letter providing these details. She offered the names of several Army officers and others who could vouch for her story.[157] The letter was referred to the Board of War, who permitted her to occupy part of the house where the office was kept. The board also awarded her twenty pounds' hard money a year during the pleasure of Congress would be proper.[158] While combing through Washington papers on the National Archives website, I came across a letter from George Washington to Samuel Huntington, dated December 25th, 1779. It reads:

To Samuel Huntington
Head Quarters Morristown 25th Decr 1779.

Sir

I have the honor to lay before your Excellency the representation of a certain Elizabeth Burgin late an inhabitant of New-York. From the testimony of different persons, and particularly many of our own officers who have returned from captivity, it would appear, that she has been indefatigable, for the relief of the prisoners, and in measures for facilitating their escape. In consequence of this conduct she incurred the suspicions of the enemy, and was finally compelled to make her escape, under the distressed circumstances which she describes. I could not forbear recommending to consideration a person who has risked so much, and been so friendly to our officers and privates, especially as to this we must attribute her present situation.

From the sense I entertained of her services and sufferings, I have ventured to take the liberty of directing the commissary at Philadelphia to furnish her and her children with rations till the pleasure of Congress could be known. Congress will judge of its justice and propriety, and how much she may be intitled to further notice.[159]

I have the honor to be with the greatest respect Your Excellency's most obt servt.[160]

Elizabeth Burgin was granted a pension by the Continental Congress for her services to the nation in 1781.

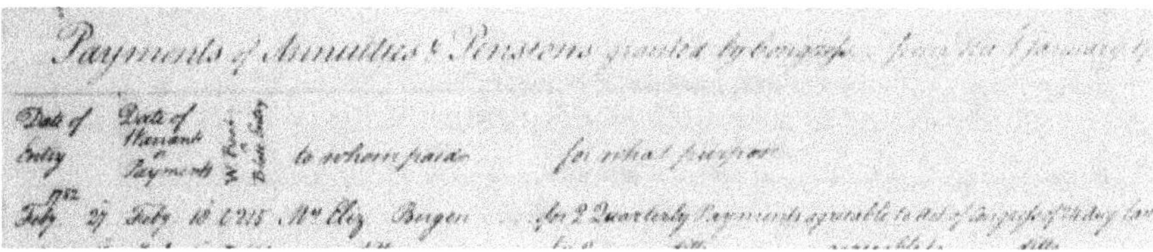

This is the petition of Elizabeth Burgin to Congress, dated July 2, 1781:

That your Petitioner was a resident of New York, where she possessed everything comfortable about her, till the summer 1779 when she was rendered so obnoxious to the British Commanders, by her exertions in the service of the American Prisoners there, that she was at first under the necessity of concealing herself, & afterwards of flying in disguise to the people, an attachment to whose cause, had reduced her to a situation so unsuitable to her sex & age. What those exertions are, the services she rendered her country were, she leaves to be told by others. Mr. Franklin & General McDougall are not unacquainted with them, & His Excellency General Washington was sensible of them. That he addressed Congress in her favor, and at the same time gave her an Order to draw Rations for herself and; three small Children, till the pleasure of Congress was known. The Letter was referred to the Board of War, who kindly permitted her to occupy part of the House where the Office is kept, & have in some other respects assisted her, but her chief Dependance being on getting her rations, which from the scarcity of provisions, she could not at all times obtain, she was often obliged to sell part of what little property she had left to remove the misery and want of her hapless Family. As she wishes not to be troublesome or expensive to the United States, she humbly conceives if the Honble Congress would be pleased to direct her full employment in cutting out the linen into shirts, purchased in this city for the Army, it would afford her a maintenance, until a happy change of affairs will permit her to return with safety to her native place."[161]

The firsthand knowledge provided clearly proved that this individual existed and was a true hero. Sadly, I cannot locate any documentation as to when Elizabeth died.

> ***"Poor is the nation that has no heroes,***
> ***but poorer still is the nation that having heroes,***
> ***fails to remember and honor them."***
> **—Marcus Tullius Cicero**

GRACE AND RACHEL MARTIN

In 1781, Major General Nathanael Greene entered South Carolina with plans to control the backcountry; the siege lasted 28 days (May 22 to June 18, 1781). This was the most prolonged field siege of the American Revolution. The Ninety-Six (the Star Fort) in the Edgefield district was located near a small town in Greenwood, SC. This location was a central part of the British strongholds designed to seal off Charles Town from the French, Spanish, as well as attacks from neighboring Indigenous tribes. By 1780, Ninety-Six had become a star-shaped military post of British provincials and Loyalist militia. Ninety-Six was critical for the defense of the northwest portion of the state and the most strategically important position in South Carolina after Camden.[162] It is estimated that there were 550 Loyalists commanded by British Lieutenant Colonel John Harris Cruger (commander from 1776-1783).

The Patriots lay siege to the city using siege line trenches and structures built for the use of the besieging army and its artillery, which were designed by the Continental Army's noted engineering talent Andrzej Tadeusz Bonawentura Kościuszko (Polish military engineer) and are considered the best example of that time period. General Greene and his Polish engineer attempted to tunnel under the Ninety-Six and pack it with black powder, and once ignited it would blow a massive hole in the fort. The walls would just crumble. In a last desperate tactic the Patriots charged the fort and failed miserably. General Greene abandoned the tunnel idea because he feared more British reinforcements would soon join the battle. On June 18th, Greene retreated to fight other battles in South Carolina. In the end the Patriots had an estimated 185 casualties, the British only had a mere seventy-five for the Loyalist defenders. Nathanael Greene stated, "The approaches have gone on exceeding slow. The British fortifications are so strong, and the garrisons so large and so well furnished, that our success is very doubtful."

While this courageous siege was taking place two sisters-in-law, Grace (maiden name Warning) and Rachel (maiden name Clay), were listening to the cries of battle from their farmhouse. These two wives were in their late teens. Grace and Rachel Martin married two of the Martin brothers, William and Barkly Martin. Both husbands were off fighting with Major Nathanael Greene. The mother of the two husbands was Mrs. Elizabeth Martin.[163] All seven of her sons were fighting in the Revolutionary War. She was quoted as saying, "They went with the spirits of Sparta go boys and fight for our country. Fight till death if you must; but never let your country be dishonored. Where I am an I would go with you."

By the time Charleston was besieged (March 29 to May 12, 1780), Mrs. Martin had three sons remaining in the war. The wives (Grace and Rachel) of the two eldest remained at home with their mother-in-law during their absence. One evening intelligence came to them that a courier traveling from Augusta to Ninety-Six conveyed important dispatches to one of the British upper stations that was to pass that night along the road unguarded by the British. Grace and Rachel mustered the courage to dress in their husbands' clothes disguised as Rebels and loaded their pistols and muskets. The two women came up with a plan to ambush the party and obtain possession of those papers at the risk of their lives. Knowing the route at which the courier would take, they ran out in the dead of night and took their station at the point on the road, which they knew the escort must pass. They had not waited long before they heard horses approaching.

I could only imagine the anxiety these heroines were feeling, standing in the dark, awaiting the approach of the enemy and the critical moment on which so much depended upon them completing their mission. The forest solitude around them, the silence of the night, and the darkness must have added to the terrors conjured up in their minds. Suddenly the courier appeared with his attendant guards. As the British courier and his escorts came closer, the women sprang from

Messrs. Goupil have also published another large engraving, entitled Elizabeth Grace and Rachel Martin. The engraving represents these two women as dressed in their husband's clothes, with horse pistols in their hands, capturing two British officers, and a courier, who was conveying some important despatches to the enemy. The heroines secured the papers, the men yielding prompt submission to the seeming soldiers. The scene is taken from Mrs. Ellet's "Women of the American Revolution."

Source: *New York Daily Herald, Newspapers.com,* 6 June 1853

the bushes, presented their pistols at the officers, and demanded the instant surrender of the party and their dispatches. The men were taken entirely by surprise and their alarm at the sudden attack yielded a prompt submission.[164] The seeming soldiers (Grace and Rachel) took possession of the papers and hurried home buy a shortcut through the woods. No time was lost in sending the necessary documents by a trustee messenger to General Greene. The venture had a singular termination. There is no mention as to who the trusted messenger was.

The British patrol returned to the road they had taken and stopped at the house of Mrs. Martin and asked for a combination as weary travelers for the night. The hostess, Grace Rachel, and Mrs. Martin inquired as to why the courier and his escorts returned so soon after they had passed. They replied by showing their paroles, saying two rebel lads had taken them prisoners. Little did these British soldiers know that they were telling their stories to the very individuals who captured them. One of the women asked, "Had you no arms?" The officers answered that they had arms; however, they had been suddenly taken off their guard and were allowed no time to use their weapons. The British soldiers departed the next morning, having no suspicion that they owed their captor to the very women whose hospitality they had claimed. Sadly, a while later William, Grace's husband, fell at the siege of Augusta, Georgia (September 15, 1780). Not long after Williams' death, a British officer made his way to Elizabeth Martins' house. He asked Mrs. Martin if she had not a son in the army at Augusta. With such hatred for the rebellion, the British officer said to the poor old mother, "I saw his brains blown out on the battlefield." The officer anticipated the mother would cry out in sorrow. But the effect of the startling announcement was other than he expected. After listening to the dreadful story, the mother's only reply was that "he could not have died in a noble or cause." The officer turned away and rode off, dissatisfied with her response.

These two women did a spontaneous act of bravery in intercepting this vital correspondence. There is no evidence as to whether Rachel or Grace came up with the idea or they both looked at each other and spontaneously came up with the same idea. They did not hesitate to jump into action an attempt to do their part in fighting against an occupying force. The definition of bravery is someone who is courageous in behavior or caracter. These women fit that definition.

JANE BLACK THOMAS

Jane was born in 1723 in Pennsylvania. Jane was married to Colonel John Thomas, commander of the Patriots' Spartan militia (1775), in South Carolina. Jane was the mother to nine children. Around 1776, Governor Edward Rutledge of South Carolina sent kegs of gunpowder, ammunition, and weapons cache to Colonel Thomas' house for safekeeping. In 1780, Colonel Thomas discovered that Tory Colonel Patrick Moore and his 150 militiamen planned an attack on Thomas' home. Colonel Thomas and his soldiers took as much ammunition and weapons that they could carry and abandoned his house, leaving Mrs. Thomas with her children, her son-in-law, and a few women to guard the remaining supply of gunpowder that was left behind. Mrs. Thomas and the unknown women barricaded themselves within the house. Soon the Tories advanced, attempting to gain entry. Jane, the women, her son-in-law, and her young sons loaded their weapons and began to fire upon the enemy. According to historian Ilene Cornwell, in her book *Three South Carolina Sites Associated with Revolutionary "Feminist" Jane Black Thomas,* the Tories began a final assault on the home. Before the Tories could go forward, Jane advanced in front of them, with a sword in her hand, and dared them to come on.[165] The Loyalist militia retreated and gathered their wounded men and ran off, not knowing that they were defeated by women and children.[166] The Tories went off and pillaged nearby homes for food, cattle, horses, took slaves, and anything else of sufficient value to take.

In 1779 Colonel Thomas of the Spartan Regiment was captured and imprisoned for fourteen months in Charleston. While Jean's husband was in jail before he was transferred to Charleston, she paid him a few visits. On one of those visits, she overheard a conversation between some Tory women who stated that the Loyalist militia intends to surprise the Rebels' camp at Cedar Springs the next night. Jane's adult children were stationed at Cedar Spring, so she rode sixty miles on horseback (in one day) to warn and pass along this vital intelligence to stop the surprise attack. This woman outrode Paul Revere, his total distance 12.5 miles, to warn the militia in the first battle of the American Revolutionary War. The Whigs knew that they were outnumbered with only sixty Whigs and fifty Loyalist militia. The Whigs knew that the number of militia forces were not on

National Number....*5718*.. State Number....*493*

APPLICATION FOR MEMBERSHIP
ISSUED BY AUTHORITY OF THE NATIONAL BOARD OF TRUSTEES

TO THE BOARD OF MANAGERS OF

THE..........South Carolina..........SOCIETY
OF THE

SONS OF THE AMERICAN REVOLUTION

I,....John B. Cannon, Sr.,..being of the age of....46....years

hereby apply for membership in this Society by right of lineal descent in the following line from ....

..............................Colonel John Thomas Sr.

who was born in....Cardiff, Wales....................on the....5....day of....April....17 20

and died in....Greenville District, S. C.....on the....21....day of....Feb.....1790

and who assisted in establishing American Independence.

I was born in....................Spartanburg....................County of....Spartanburg

State of....South Carolina....................on the....31....day of....July....1889

(1) I am the son of......Erastus V. Cannon....................born 1856, died Dec 1893, and

his wife....Nancy Aurelia Fant....................born Dec 12 1861, died 6/10/17, married 11/14/8

(2) grandson of Major John Alexander Fant....................born 4/3/1842, died 6/20/93, and

his wife....Sarah Jane McJunkin....................born 5/13/31, died 6/14/97, married 10/29/5

(3) great-grandson of Joseph McJunkin Jr.....................born 10/8/1791, died 2/27/50, and

his wife....Nany Sartor....................born 1796, died 1853, married 1815

(4) great-great-grandson of....Major Joseph McJunkin....................born 6/22/1125, died 5/31/1846, and

his wife....Ann Thomas....................born 1/15/1748, died 3/17/1626, married 3/9/1799

(5) great-great-great-grandson of....Col. John Thomas, Sr.,....................born 4/5/1724, died 3/21/1790, and

his wife....Jane Black....................born 7/3/1722, died 6/12/1750, married 1/3/1740

(6) great-great-great-great-grandson of....................born....................died....................and

his wife....................born....................died....................married....................

(7) great-great-great-great-great-grandson of....................born....................died....................and

his wife....................born....................died....................married....................

and he, the said....Col. John Thomas, Sr.....................(No. 5) is the ancestor who assisted in

establishing American Independence, while acting in the capacity of....Colonel of the Spartan

....Regiment organized Sept 11 1775 member of Provincial Congress which

....first met in Jan. 1775 in Charleston, S. C.

Nominated and recommended by the undersigned members of the Society	Signature of applicant, (Name in full)
[signature]	*John Burns Cannon*
[signature]	Address,
[signature]	304 Andrews Bldg. Spartanburg, S. C.
[signature]	Occupation, Special Agent New York Life Ins. Co.

COLONEL JOHN THOMAS SR.

COLONEL JOHN THOMAS SR. was born near Cardiff, Wales, April 5th, 1720, and with his parents came to America, settling in Chester County, Pennsylvania, July 20th, 1725. On January 3rd, 1740, he married Jane Black, the sister of Rev. John Black, first president of Dickinson College. She was born July 8th, 1723, near Carlisle, Pennsylvania, where they were married. On December 20th 1749, he went to South Carolina, settling on Fishing Creek, in Chester District. In November, 1762, he removed to Spartanburg District (now Spartanburg County) and made his home on Fair Forest Creek.

Between the years of 1755 and 1775 he held commissions as magistrate and Captain of Militia under the Royal Government, but at the beginning of hostilities between the Colonies and England he resigned these commissions and was elected COLONEL OF THE SPARTAN REGIMENT, ORGANIZED SEPT. 11, 1775. HE WAS A MEMBER OF THE PROVINCIAL CONGRESS which first met in January, 1775, in Charleston, S.C. On March 26, 1776, the Provincial Congress resolved into a General Assembly. There fore Colonel Thomas was a member of the first congress and the first general assembly in the Province of South Carolina. He retained the command of the Spartan Regiment until after the fall of Charlestown, in May, 1780. He was arrested by the Tory leader, Sam Brown, and sent to prison at Ninety-six, and from there to Charleston, where he remained until the close of the war. After his father's capture, John Thomas, Jr., became Colonel of the Spartan Regiment, with rendez-vous at Cedar Springs, South Carolina. Mrs. Thomas visited her husband in prison while at Ninety-Six, where their two sons were also prisoners. By chance she overheard some Tory women talking. One said: "Tomorrow night the Loyalists are going to surprise the Rebels at Cedar Springs." In this camp were some of her own sons. Riding sixty miles on horseback to warn the friends at camp, measures of defense were taken, and when the enemy arrived that night they charged a camp with fires burning brightly but totally empty. The Patriots fired from the rear and the attacking party missed annihilation at their hands. This affair took place on July 12, 1780.

"Sometime early in the war, Governor Rutledge sent a quantity of arms and ammunition to the house of Colonel Thomas, to be in readiness for any emergency that might arise on the frontier. The house was prepared to resist assault, and put under the guard of twenty-five men. Intelligence was received by Colonel Thomas that a large party of Tories led by Colonel Moore, of North Carolina, was advancing to attack him. Thomas and his guard considered it unwise to risk an engagement with a force so much larger than their own; consequently, they withdrew to a place of safety, carrying as much of the ammunition with them as possible. Josiah Culbertson, a son-in-law of Thomas, belonged to the guard, but refusing to leave the house with the others. He and little William Thomas were the only occupants of the house, except the women. At length Moore and his band appeared before the house and prepared for the capture of the booty, which did not turn out to be such an easy task. Their demand for admittance was answered by an order to leave the place. The old-fashioned "batten door" strongly barricaded, resisted their efforts to demolish it, and their fire did little or no execution because of the heavy logs of which the house was built. Their fire proved to be much more effective than that of the assailants. Mrs. Thomas and her daughters, aided by the youthful William, loaded the guns as fast as Culbertson could fire them. Culbertson, being an expert marksman, was doing so much execution, and the rapidity with which the guns were fired, led the enemy to believe that a considerable force was concealed in the house, and that further effort was useless. Getting things together, Moore and his crowd

Jane Black Thomas

their side and they decided to lay in hiding behind their campfires and when the Loyalist militia arrived in the dead of night, being so confident of their victory, the Whigs attacked them and were victorious in their minor skirmish against the Loyalist militia.

According to family historian Jennifer Beckett (noted on *ancestry.com*), Jane steadily refused to drink any tea after the Revolutionary War. Jane often said it was the blood of some of the poor men and women who first fell in the war.[167] She remained a Patriot until her death in 1811.

Historians did Jane Black an injustice by excluding her as one of the most famous persons who alerted the Colonial militia of an impending British attack. By omitting Jane Black's and other women's courageous efforts, it demonstrates a real problem regarding gender imbalance when it comes to historians integrating women into history.

MARY ALDIS DRAPER

Mary Draper was born on December 4, 1719, in Norfolk County, Massachusetts. Both her parents were also born in Norfolk, Massachusetts. Her first husband was Allen Abel Jr., who died in 1739. They had three children. Mary remarried in 1743 to Moses Draper III, where she had seven more children with her second husband.[168] Mary lived in Massachusetts at the time when she heard about the war raging on. Mary believed that for America to be free, it had to go to war with Great Britain. She was a compassionate woman who always helped those in need. And now, the Continental soldiers and Patriot militia would be in dire need of her assistance. She encouraged her husband (Captain Draper) and her eldest son to join the Continental Army (her husband died in January 1775).[169] They did not hesitate. Captain Draper and his son joined Gardiner's Massachusetts Regiment, the 25th Continental Regiment. After her husband and son left, Mary's family started to do their part in the war.

Her family made cloth from their possessions into coats for the Colonial soldiers; sheets and blankets were made into shirts, and flannel already made up into her clothes was turned into men's clothing. She also set up a food table by the road to hand out food like cheese and bread, and old John brought cider to the troops as they passed by. Mary once said, *"Food must be prepared for the hungry; for before tomorrow night hundreds, I hope thousands, will be on their way to join the Continental forces."* When her food supply began to run low, she called upon her neighbors to assist her with feeding the troops as they pass by. Thankfully many of her neighbors were kind enough to contribute.[170]

After the battle of Bunker Hill (June 17, 1775), General Washington called upon his fellow Americans that his troops' ammunition and to send every ounce of lead or pewter at their disposal, *saying that any quantity, however small, would be gratefully received.* Mary followed General Washington's orders and melted her precious pewter her departed mother gifted her, her platters, pans, and dishes into bullets for the patriotic cause.

It was also known that Mary opened her house to those who became destitute due to the war. Mary survived two husbands and one war. She died in 1810.

According to her family, Mary was an overall sweet and caring woman. There is a DAR chapter located in Wichita, KS, dedicated to Mary Draper. Strangely this chapter was formed in 2017.

DAR medal

Mary Aldis Draper – Great Woman of the American Revolution

"It is high time society change
their barbaric way of thinking towards women."
- Juanita Stellato Maldonado

MOLLY SCOTT

Who is the true hero of Fort Henry? Was it Elizabeth "Betty Zane" McLaughlin Clark or Molly Scott? Before we can understand who Molly Scott was, let us talk about the events that led up to Molly's heroic deed. After Lord Cornwallis had surrendered to General Washington on October 19, 1781, a detachment of fifty British Loyalists in a military unit called the Queen's Rangers, commanded by Simon Girty and a Captain Pratt, along with three hundred Seneca, Shawnee, and Wyandot Indigenous peoples, laid a second siege to Fort Henry in Delaware, Ohio (September 1782). As a child, Girty was captured by an Indigenous tribe and grew up in their society, gaining notoriety for his savagery toward settlers. This siege is because the colonists disobeyed the royal order that land west of the Appalachian Mountains was reserved for Indigenous tribes. Did Girty not hear that Lord Cornwallis surrendered in 1781, or was he acting out vengeance on behalf of the Indigenous tribes? The French surrendered to the British their claims of the Appalachian Mountains, Mississippi River, and Canada. In 1763, King George III signed a Royal Proclamation (The Proclamation Line), which drew an imaginary line along the eastern seaboard following the Appalachian Mountains.

The British government proclaimed this line to be the furthest westward point of permissible Colonial expansion. The proclamation stated that any Colonist that lived within this imaginary line had to vacate by order of the king immediately. Superior Officer Colonel David Shepherd with the Continental Army was charged with defending the fort. His troops consisted of forty men and boys charged with protecting an estimated sixty women and children from the surrounding area who had come to the fort for protection. Colonel Shepherd refused to surrender. The settlers were prepared to fight to the death. They became accustomed to the history of violence between the Indigenous tribes and settlers. The Patriots defended Fort Henry bravely, which resulting in victory for the Patriots and settlers. However, they almost lost the battle when the gunpowder started to run low and they would soon not be able to defend the fort. And that is where the story starts to become a little muffled. Some historians claim that Elizabeth Betty Zane was the sixteen-year-old girl who volunteered to retrieve gunpowder from Colonel Ebenezer Zane's cabin (who was killed in the siege days prior). It is said that Betty ran sixty yards to fetch the gunpowder. She placed the gunpowder in her apron and ran back to the fort so the Patriots can win the battle.

Other historians claim that a young woman named Molly Scott (full name unknown) was the true hero. Historical facts and legends are intermingled regarding the story as to which young woman carried the gunpowder in her apron. The first known published account of Betty Zane's brave gun-pottering exploit appeared in a novel written by her great-great-nephew Pearl Zane Grey, titled *Ohio River Trilogy,* published in 1903. Mr. Grey was an American author who wrote adventure novels pertaining to the Wild West and provided no evidence to his claim nor any historical facts.

In 1969 a newspaper published by *The Times Recorder* in Ohio by Norris F. Schneider, titled "Betty Zane's Daring Dash Saved Settlers at Wheeling," states that Betty was in Pennsylvania living with her father attending Quaker school at the time of the siege. In the early 1900s an attorney named James Taylor Holmes decided to investigate the legend of Betty Zane. In a 1964 news article in *The Times Recorder* by Norris Schneider titled "Behind Betty Zane Legend," states that attorney Holmes found no tangible evidence that states Betty Zane was the young woman who carried the gunpowder and that the story heavily relied on secondary sources such as newspaper articles and witness statements from Zane's relatives.

There are no known official records of Betty Zane participating in the first or second attacks on Fort Henry. On November 28, 1849, a Lydia Boggs (who was at Fort Henry) signed an affidavit proclaiming that Molly Scott, wife of Fort Henry defender Andrew Scott, had made the famous gunpowder run to save Wheeling's Fort Henry during the 1782 siege, and not Betty Zane, had transported the vital gunpowder during the 1782 siege of Fort Henry. Historians claim that Mrs. Boggs was a childhood friend of Betty Zane and was jealous of her and signed the affidavit out of spite. However, that is hearsay and not evidentiary.

Lydia Boggs' official declaration states the following:

> *During the forenoon of Tuesday, September 12th, the enemy having temporarily withdrawn from the attack but occupying a position within gunshot of the fort, those within the stockade*

observed a female leave the residence of Colonel Zane and advance with rapid movement toward the fort. She made for the Southern gate, as it was less exposed to the fire of the enemy. The gate was opened immediately, and she entered in safety. That person was none other than Molly Scott, and the object of her mission was to procure powder for those who defended the dwelling of Colonel Zane!

This is a case of stolen valor. Wills DeHass included Boggs' affidavit in his book, *History of the Early Settlement and Indian Wars of Western Virginia*, published in 1851.[171] Zane's role is widely accepted by historians, so therefore the claims of Molly Scott being the heroine is dismissed. The powder incident remained a mystery until 2003, when the Ebenezer Zane Chapter of the National Society Sons of the American Revolution placed a new marker on the grave of Molly Scott (September 20th), bestowing the honor upon Molly Scott, as one of the brave women who helped to defend Fort Henry.

Past historians were mistaken, and the credit should properly be given to Molly Scott. She was the true heroine. It is highly unlikely that there were two gunpowder exploits at the same time. However, what if they both were heroines but at different times, one possibly in 1777 with Molly Scott as the heroine and another in 1782 with Betty Zane?

Source: Photo by Treni Vucelich

ROSANNA WATERS FARROW

Rosanna was born in Virginia 1734. In 1751 she married John Thomas Farrow and had five sons; three of them joined the Continental Army (around 1780) and four daughters. In 1776, Mr. Farrow died of smallpox in North Carolina, leaving Rosanna to raise her boys all alone. Rosanna was a Patriot who lived in South Carolina; she was surrounded by Tory neighbors, who knew that she was in support of the Patriot cause. In 1897, a Ruth Petty wrote an essay about Rosanna. In the essay she stated the family was forced into many cruel straits in order that the family might have food. For example, often they were obliged to hide it in hollow trees and among the rocky coves of the Enorree (located in Spartanburg County) and were even forced sometimes to shelter themselves among the woods and swamps when it was too dangerous to return home. They slept with weapons under their pillows, for they never knew at what secret watch of the night they might be summoned to their doors by the enemy.

What makes Rosanna a heroine is that she ransomed all three of her sons from execution by the British with six of their own soldiers. In the *Macon Telegraph* newspaper, published in 1917, it states that one night a rider came by her house and shouted a message, saying, *"Three of your sons are prisoners at Ninety-six, and that British Lt. Colonel John Harris Cruger will exchange one rebel for two British regulars. All will be shot who are not exchanged."* Cruger commanded the defense of fort Ninety-Six in 1781.[172] After hearing the devastating news, the mother acted. I mean honestly, wouldn't you? No doubt in my mind every parent would have done the same thing. She rode alone through the night to the Patriots camp (Fair Forest) to request from Colonel James Henderson Williams six British prisoners to be given in exchange for three of her sons, captured in battle, and who were to be executed.[173] Colonel Williams agreed, gave her what she demanded and a guard.

Off she quickly rode from Fair Forest to fort Ninety-six . Took her two days to arrive, praying that she was not too late to save her boys. When she was able to see the Ninety-six fort, she took her apron and waited it as a truce flag (white flag). The British Colonel Curger saying, *"Just in time I was going to execute your sons at sunrise. But I will carry out my agreement."* Her boys were freed.

Rosanna hand one last word to give the British Colonel: *"I have given you two for one, Colonel Cruger, but understand that I consider it the best trade I ever made, for rest assured hereafter the 'Farrow boys' will whip you four to one."* [174]

For as long as she lived, she was admired and loved, and it is said that even years after the eyes of the British soldiers flashed with pleasure when they talked of this event in South Carolina. Rosanna died in 1800 in South Carolina.

**"A woman is like a tea bag;
you never know how strong it is until it's in hot water."
—Eleanor Roosevelt**

SYBIL LUDINGTON

Sybil Ludington was born in 1761 New York and was the eldest of twelve. Her parents were Colonel Henry, who was the commander of a local militia, and Abigail Ludington. Like many in Colonial America her family were farmers, and she would tend to the farm and her younger sibling.

Sybil was recognized as a heroine of the American Revolutionary War. When asking many of my peers who she was they could not answer the question, but they could recognize the name. In 1777 the British launched a new strategy to divide the colonies by seizing centrally located New York and all their harbors and cutting off New England. With an estimated force of two thousand men, British, on April 26th, 1777, General William Tryon targeted a Continental Army supplies store in Danbury, Connecticut, just 25 miles from the family home. While the British were attempting to locate the supply store, they looted and set the entire town ablaze. The militia at Danbury was only one hundred and fifty strong and was forced to withdraw. A Patriot messenger from Danbury fled the fighting and was ordered to seek out the nearest militia, located in Fredericksburg, New York, to alert them of the British assault and to help fight the aggressors. Colonel Henry Ludington (French and Indian War veteran), commander of the Seventh Regiment of the Duchess County, New York, militia, with four hundred militiamen under his command, was notified. Colonel Ludington had to gather his militiamen and other nearby militia units to stop the Redcoats from advancing. The Colonel feared that if the British and Tory forces reached the Hudson River, they would cut off the colonies' communications. The Colonel had to organize a battle plan and could not make the journey himself. You see, this was planting season and many of the militia men went back to their farms to plant crops (sorry, people, no grocery stores). This meant someone had to go to each house and rally up the militia.

That is when his daughter Sybil (age sixteen) volunteered for the task. Her father was reluctant because she was a sixteen-year-old girl, and the ride would be dangerous. Everyone in American elementary school is taught that Paul Revere raised the alarm that the "Regulars" were coming before the battle of Lexington and Concord (April 19, 1775). However, nothing about Sybil. Like William Dawes and Samuel Prescott, other riders warned nearby towns that the

"Regulars" (Redcoats) were coming. Revere only rode twelve miles to warn the militia at Lexington, whereas Sybil rode forty. Sybil Ludington (a year after Revere's ride), knowing the trails and the roadways, rode forty miles all night in the countryside through the mud and rain to gather her father's militia and neighbors to fight the Redcoats in Danbury to stop them from advancing further. Not only did the weather suck, Sybil also had to avoid cowboys and skinners, a vigilante-like bands of militia who were Raiders that operated in the neutral ground, which was known as the Hudson Territory from 1776 until the end of the war. These not-so-pleasant men harassed the local citizens and indiscriminately stole from both Loyalists and Patriots. It is noted that Sybil yelled and banged on the doors with a stick: *"The British are burning Danbury! Muster at Ludington's (Colonel Ludington's house)! By Daybreak!"* Four hundred militiamen arrived at her father's house. Colonel Ludington led his militia to Connecticut, where they drove the British troops to Long Island.

There are several children's books and small paperbacks written about Sybil. However, when I am thumbing through famous Revolutionary War history books, I see no mention of her. Only of Paul Revere. Many of these small paperback books try to romanticize Sybil. Sad, historians should stick to the facts and not be biased or prejudiced against the individual writing about. However, as you read in this book, that is impossible for many male historians to do.

Eighty-five years after Paul Revere's famous ride, Henry Wadsworth Longfellow wrote a poem (1860) titled "Paul Revere's Ride," which immortalized Revere. Both of these men were prominent American poets; however, Paul Revere's poem is the most notable throughout historians. I wonder why that is. Perhaps because he did not have a uterus. Yeah, I think that is the reason. Sybil should be recognized as the female Paul Revere. However, why compare her to him since he was outridden by her? By comparing her to Paul Revere, historians give him more recognition because of his name. Sybil did her duty and did not seek fame like Revere. We must correct history and note that Paul Revere was not the only one who rode miles to warn others that *the Redcoats were coming.*

Sybil later married Edmond Ogden and had one son. Sybil died in 1839; she is buried at Patterson Presbyterian Church Cemetery in New York. In 1940 there

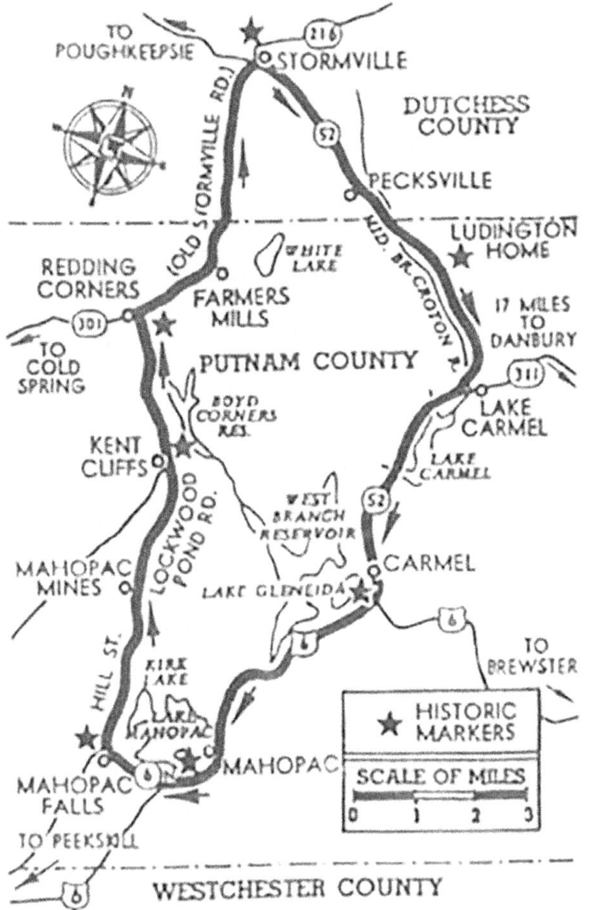

The probable route of Sybil Ludington's night ride through what is now Putnam County, New York.

Source: Hudson River Valley Institute
The probable route of Sybil Ludington's night ride through what is now Putnam County, NY

was a poem written by Burton Braley titled "Sybil Ludington's Ride." However, Braley's poem did not immortalize Sybil. Below is that poem:

Listen, my children, and you shall hear
Of a lovely feminine Paul Revere
Who rode an equally famous ride
Through a different part of the countryside,
Where Sybil Ludington's name recalls
A ride as daring as that of Paul's.
In April, Seventeen Seventy-Seven,
A smoky glow in the eastern heaven
(A fiery herald of war and slaughter)
Came to the eyes of the Colonel's daughter.
"Danbury's burning," she cried aloud.
The Colonel answered, "'Tis but a cloud,
A cloud reflecting the campfires red,
So hush you, Sybil, and go to bed."
"I hear the sound of the cannon drumming"
"'Tis only the wind in the treetops humming!
So go to bed, as a young lass ought,
And give the matter no further thought."
Young Sybil sighed as she turned to go,
"Still, Danbury's burning—that I know.[175]*"*
Sound of a horseman riding hard
Clatter of hoofs in the manor yard
Feet on the steps and a knock resounding
As a fist struck wood with a mighty pounding.
The doors flung open, a voice is heard,
"Danbury's burning—I rode with word;
Fully half of the town's gone
And the British—the British are coming on.
Send a messenger, get our men!"
His message finished the horseman then

Juanita Stellato Maldonado

Staggered wearily to a chair
And fell exhausted in slumber there.
The Colonel muttered, "And who, my friend,
Is the messenger I can send?
Your strength is spent and you cannot ride
And then, you know not the countryside;
I cannot go for my duty's clear;
When my men come in they must find me here;
There's devil a man on the place tonight
To warn my troopers to come-and fight.
Then, who is my messenger to be?"
Said Sybil Ludington, "You have me."
"You!" said the Colonel, and grimly smiles,
"You! My daughter, you're just a child."
"Child!" cried Sybil. "Why I'm sixteen!
My mind's alert and my senses keen,
I know where the trails and the roadways are
And I can gallop as fast and far
As any masculine rider can.
You want a messenger? I'm your Man!"
The Colonel's heart was aglow with pride.
"Spoke like a soldier. Ride, girl, ride
Ride like the devil; ride like sin;
Summon my slumbering troopers in.
I know when duty is to be done
That I can depend on a Ludington!"
So over the trails to the towns and farms
Sybil delivered the call to arms.
Riding swiftly without a stop
Except to rap with a riding crop
On the soldiers' doors, with a sharp tattoo
And a high-pitched feminine halloo.
"Up! Up there, soldier. You're needed, come!

The British are marching!" and then the drum
Of her horse's feet as she rode apace
To bring more men to the meeting place.

In this chapter your learned that Paul Revere only rode 12.5 miles, whereas Sybil Ludington road forty, Jane black Thomas sixty, and Ann Bailey 160 miles to warn and gather the militia for battles. However, historians failed to make this comparison. Here is a breakdown:

Paul Revere	12.5	to warn the militia in the first battle of the American Revolutionary War.	
Sibyl Ludington	40	to gather her father's militia neighbors to fight the Redcoats Danbury to stop them from advancing further.	
Jane Black Thomas	60	to warn and pass along this intelligence to stop the surprise attack.	60 miles in one day
Anne Bailey	160	rode from one recruiting station to another, she also volunteered as a frontier messenger for the colonial forces, she frequently traveled	Rode between Fort Savannah (now Lewisburg) and Fort Randolph at Point Pleasant.

"Men make the moral code and they expect women to accept it.
They have decided that it is entirely right and proper
for men to fight for their liberties and their rights,
but that it is not right and proper for women to fight for theirs"
—Emmeline Pankhurst

CHAPTER 6
The King Has Fallen

The French, Dutch and Spanish governments entered the War of Independence because they had a common enemy. With three countries united, it would benefit all economic interests, so they thought it best to become allies with North America. The Revolutionary War was not fought because of economics alone, or to put the founding fathers in charge; the main objective of the Americans was to stop the brutality the British troops put upon those who lived in the thirteen colonies. British troops tormented colonists, raped women, beat the poor, hung children for stealing food, and burned farms all because they could. During the American Revolution, America's population was estimated at three million, of whom half were slaves. Colonists were fighting to end oppression by a monarchy who ruled them with an iron fist, who lived thousands of miles away. Extraordinary people had to break out of their social constraints to fight for freedom. So, the question is how one of the most significant military powers in the world was defeated by a few million scattered, inadequately armed, and poorly trained colonials. To win a conflict, ordinary people suddenly developed the courage and strength to take up arms against a foreign enemy. Many of the unnamed heroes of the American Revolutionary War did not stop to think of the psychological implications war might cause them. When war is knocking at your door, many who answered did not consider the consequences. Soldiers picked up their gear, packed their belongings, kissed their wives, and ran out the door. The American militia adopted Native fighting tactics, new the layout of the land, the passion of resisting a superpower and, well, the British were overconfident and underestimated their opponents as a bunch of farmers with pitchforks. Without the common people's will to stand up against oppression the ideal of a free equal land, it would have disappeared into dust.

Many Americans assume that King George was the main villain in the Revolutionary War. Parliament, Prime Minister Frederick North, and other ministers were the primary policymakers. The British Empire pursued a desire to win the war versus the illogical strategic goal of winning over the people they wish to rule over. They failed to recognize that you will not win the war if you do not win over the people. By the middle of the war, King George was persistent and wanted to continue the fight. As the war progressed, British Generals were arguing amongst themselves, stating that this war was impossible to win, and Frederick North wished to resign from the war. The king argued if Great Britain lost America, Britain would be viewed as no longer a superpower. That is not to say that King George had not influenced the causes of the American Revolution. In November 1774, the king stated to Lord North, *"We must either master them or totally leave them to themselves."* Britain had a depleted their army (cost played a factor); however, it did have the world's largest navy. At the beginning of the war, the British Army had an estimated 45,000 men spread worldwide, protecting their empires. Britain had their troops in the Caribbean, Gibraltar, the French War (1778), and the island of Minorca; British forces were in small numbers in the thirteen colonies. As we can recall, King George III thought this rebellion of disobedient children would be over in a matter of days or weeks. With a small number of forces to fight the Revolutionary War, the rebellion was quickly won. Additionally, British generals failed to study the terrain of their enemy. With their troops spread thin, British forces were in small numbers in the thirteen colonies. There were around 22,000 soldiers in North America, and another estimated 25,000 to 30,000 faithful Loyalists to Great Britain. However, Britain alone did not take up arms against the rebellious colonists; Landgraf Friedrich II of Germany sent an estimated 30,000 mercenaries called Hessians, who served as auxiliaries in support of the British Army. The British military had poor planning and lacked cooperation. One example is that British General John Burgoyne came up with a strategy to take the Hudson River (1777), which ran to New York and Canada.

The objective was to isolate New England from all the other colonies and stop supplies going to the South, which Burgoyne believed would strangle the American rebellion into submission. This plan involved 8,000 to 9,000 troops that would invade Canada. Burgoyne was triumphant and captured Fort Ticonderoga in June 1777; however, Burgoyne strained his supply chain. The Patriot militia took notice and cut off Burgoyne's supply line, resulting in General Burgoyne being defeated in Vermont and New York. General Sir Henry Clinton departed New York to assist Burgoyne with more troops. He sailed up the river to seek out and fight the Continental Army. Clinton achieved several victories by seizing control of the Hudson Highland Forts. However, he later sailed north, unable to reach Burgoyne before he retreated, and surrendered 6,000 remaining troops at Saratoga. General William Howe also attempted to take control of the Hudson River. He took a large army up the Hudson and had Commander Sir Guy Carleton travel down the Hudson River toward Canada. However, Carleton abandoned his push for Canada and turned back. This set the scene for a spectacular breakdown in cooperation between British forces, which doomed the Hudson strategy to failure.[176] British Generals eventually abandoned the taking of the Hudson River. Inadequacies and poor planning, misinformation, and poor strategic planning were the downfalls of Britain's invasion. The British attempted multiple times to take possession of the Hudson River and failed because the Continental Army and the militia fortified towns along the Hudson River, miscommunication between the British General and infighting within the British authorities. British officers often complained that their soldiers lacked discipline in many battles by rushing too impetuously toward the Continental Army and sometimes fired without given orders. Britain did not adequately train its foot soldiers and failed to study the terrain of their enemy. British troops thought that they were fighting at nothing but many farmers with pitchforks and were defined as disobedient children that must be punished. Not learning about their enemy and only trusting the Indigenous people to guide them through the uncharted territories produced strategies that failed at evolving their step-by-step instructions for carrying out battles. In the Battle of Saratoga, General John Burgoyne surrendered to General Horatio Gates on October 17, 1777, at Saratoga, which gave the French the green light to come into the American Revolution, followed by the Spanish, then the Dutch, and much of the rest of Europe. Burgoyne used Natives as scouts. However, they were also raiding American settlements, which helped increase support for the American cause.

Burgoyne positioned his forces to near Saratoga, NY. The actual number of troops differs on the source, and some say 9,000 American and 7,200 British. Burgoyne wanted General St. Leger and General Howe to meet up with him in Albany and, well, that did not happen. St. Leger and Howe made separate attacks at different locations. Miscommunication within the British high command and intercepted communication prevented the two commands to join Burgoyne at Saratoga. Burgoyne, low on men, decided not to man the outposts to the north, which cut himself off from his allies and supporting troops.

FAILED SOUTHERN STRATEGY

After the British lost the battle of Saratoga, the British Army turned their attention toward the South. They devised a Southern Strategy with support from Loyalists in the South. In early 1778, British Secretary Lord George Germain wrote a letter to Sir Henry Clinton, stating that capturing the Southern colonies was considered by the king as an object of great importance in the scale of the war.[177] The first plan of action was to take control of the Southern Atlantic port of Savannah, GA. With control of this port, the British would control imports to Southern plantations and the central mercantile hub. On December 29, 1778, an estimated 2,500 to 3,600 British troops (under the command of General Augustin Prévost), Hessians, and Loyalists captured the city of Savannah, Georgia, with little to no resistance. After, the British military soon captured Charleston, South Carolina (1780); this was a horrendous setback for the Continental Army and to stamp out any Colonial resistance during the Redcoats' pressing through South Carolina. At the Battle of Cowpens (January 17, 1781), the British was led by Lieutenant Colonel Sir Banastre Tarleton, who commanded approximately 1,100 soldiers.[178]

When in battle, Tarleton continuously illustrated a will to quickly close with and destroy his enemy through audacity, tempo, and often reckless fighting, and so he adapted to Tarleton's tactics.[179] The night before the battle, Tarleton gathered his men and gave the order of no quarter to the treasonous Colonials. The British lost this battle because the seventh Fusiliers held fire without orders. Tarleton and most of the British soldiers surrendered. The rest ran off like cowards to seek safer grounds. The loss of this battle was devastating to the British. This battle lasted for only one hour and was one of the most decisive

American victories of the War for Independence. Tarleton's military tactics were reckless and ruthless, and his eagerness to fight created a cocky attitude, which led to his defeat at Cowpen. Several key factors contributed to Britain's unsuccessful attempt at their Southern Strategy. Factor one: The British had two assumptions. First, the British thought there was a large number of Loyalists in the South. Moreover, the British assumed these wealthy Loyalists would be willing to fight in a militia. This was a critical miscalculation because neither Clinton nor General Cornwallis had the means for raising resources for training and equipping the Loyalists with weapons. Lord George Germain told the House of Commons that it had never been his idea that America could be conquered.[180] The British failed to see the struggle of training Loyalists who never experienced hard labor, let alone picked up a musket to fight in a militia. They would have much rather had someone else do the fighting for them. Factor two: Britain failed to recognize the connection between the different cultures that came to live in the new world. Britain was unable to accept a more contemporary population mixed with countries and various shades of people worldwide. The British had a bias thinking that they were superior to any other race because their king stated so. All parties failed to "understand and address the grievances"[181] from each other, the Loyalists, and the Patriots. They were unable to "care" about the impacts on the people socially, culturally, politically, and militarily. I agree with Jacobsen's assessment: "Civil affairs organization outside the military are vital as part of the process, for failure to synchronize the plans and objectives will weaken efforts and may cause both to fail." You cannot have a "common society" when you have people loyal to an absent king and others devoted to General Washington. Those two ideologies are toxic together in one pot, let alone one community. To rebuild, you must reintroduce an understanding that the ideological goal is to live in a free society, which is best for all citizens—freedom to live free from a totalitarian government.

Lord George Germain said the British failed in this war and later wrote a letter to General Clinton saying so. General Clinton did not have Naval support, so he abandoned his plans to capture Charleston. In 1779, Clinton had to give up 2,000 troops for Canada's battle, which stretched his army ultra-thin. By the time Clinton was to partake in the Southern Strategy, his 2,000 troops were never replaced, and he was ordered to send more reinforcements to Jamaica. This man could not win. Germain had no choice other than to abandon his push to the South and withdrew from Newport. The British Army adapted to the European environment of the time, to the political and social climate and the geography and terrain. Men knowledgeable in military matters during this era passionately believed that nobody of poorly trained citizens (Colonists), however numerous and inspired, could stand before the disciplined ranks of professionals. Today we can see many of the weaknesses in the eighteenth-century military system that was not so obvious to contemporaries (its fundamental lack of flexibility, a paucity of authentic professional leadership, and its failure to mobilize national resources for war effectively). In that case, these perceptions resulted from a vastly different social and political environment.

The Revolution's story can hardly be told in terms of long-term strategy and its success or failure. Neither side ever had any consistent plan for the conduct of the war. Most of the time the British, who retained the strategic initiative, failed to use it to great advantage. They were highly uncertain about their objective; they made plans from year to year and seldom coordinated them even for a single year. Blame for this hesitant approach falls in almost equal part on the administration in England and the British commanders in America. King George III; Lord North, his Principal Minister; and Lord George Germain, Secretary of State for the American Department, were the three British officials mainly responsible for the war's conduct. In assessing blame in this fashion, one must keep in mind the difficulties of logistics and communications under which the British labored. These difficulties made it virtually impossible to coordinate plans over great distances or assemble men and materials in time to pursue one logical and consistent strategy. The British wanted to do an internal order. Internal order would be forced upon loyal colonies. Many Loyalists were businessmen, wealthy landowners, Royal elitists, and appointees by the British Empire. Of course, they would take a pacifist standpoint in the Revolutionary War if the British decided to win them over politically versus using military might. The British assumed winning over loyal colonies by political power was a good strategy? I find that idea to be humorous. What dictatorship ever won over an entire country by only using political might? If the British decided on this tactic and this tactic alone, it would be a major miscalculation on their part. The Continental Army would not permit them to have any power within America's borders.

Problems the British faced have been either overlooked or rapidly dismissed. Still, the disadvantages from which the British commanders may have suffered do not entirely account for the British loss. The American strategy was primarily defensive and consequently had to be mainly shaped to counter British moves. [182] Uncertainties as to the supply of both men and materials acted on the American side even more effectively to thwart developing a consistent plan for winning the war.

Source: The Basics, Artist Filippo Costaggini

General George Washington, on horseback, receives the sword of surrender from Major General O'Hare, who represented Lord Cornwallis after his defeat at Yorktown, the last battle of the American Revolution. (1781)

LETTER ON THE LOSS OF AMERICA

In the 1780s King George III wrote a letter (the precise date of this letter is unknown):

America is lost! Must we fall beneath the blow? Or have we resources that may repair the mischief? What are those resources? Should they be sought in distant Regions held by precarious Tenure, or shall we seek them at home in the exertions of a new policy?

The situation of the Kingdom is novel, the policy that is to govern it must be novel likewise, or neither adapted to the real evils of the present moment, or the dreaded ones of the future.

For a Century past the Colonial Scheme has been the system that has guided the Administration of the British Government. It was thoroughly known that from every Country there always exists an active emigration of unsettled, discontented, or unfortunate People, who failing in their endeavours to live at home, hope to succeed better where there is more employment suitable to their poverty. The establishment of Colonies in America might probably increase the number of this class, but did not create it; in times anterior to that great speculation, Poland contained near 10,000 Scotch Pedlars; within the last thirty years not above 100, occasioned by America offering a more advantageous asylum for them.

A people spread over an immense tract of fertile land, industrious because free, and rich because industrious, presently became a market for the Manufactures and Commerce of the Mother Country. An importance was soon generated, which from its origin to the late conflict was mischievous to Britain, because it created an expense of blood and treasure worth more at this instant, if it could be at our command, than all we ever received from America. The wars of

1744, of 1756, and 1775, were all entered into from the encouragements given to the speculations of settling the wilds of North America.

It is to be hoped that by degrees it will be admitted that the Northern Colonies, that is those North of Tobacco, were in reality our very successful rivals in two Articles, the carrying freight trade, and the Newfoundland fishery. While the Sugar Colonies added above three millions a year to the wealth of Britain, the Rice Colonies near a million, and the Tobacco ones almost as much; those more to the north, so far from adding anything to our wealth as Colonies, were trading, fishing, farming Countries, that rivalled us in many branches of our industry, and had actually deprived us of no inconsiderable share of the wealth we reaped by means of the others. This compartative view of our former territories in America is not stated with any idea of lessening the consequence of a future friendship and connection with them; on the contrary it is to be hoped we shall reap more advantages from their trade as friends than ever we could derive from them as Colonies; for there is reason to suppose we actually gained more by them while in actual rebellion, and the common open connection cut off, than when they were in obedience to the Crown; the Newfoundland fishery taken into the Account, there is little doubt of it.

The East and West Indies are conceived to be the great commercial supports of the Empire; as to the Newfoundland fishery time must tell us what share we shall reserve of it. But there is one observation which is applicable to all three; they depend on very distant territorial possessions, which we have little or no hopes of retaining from their internal strength, we can keep them only by means of a superior Navy. If our marine force sinks, or if in consequence of wars, debts, and taxes, we should in future find ourselves so debilitated as to be involved in a new War, without the means of carrying it on with vigour, in these cases, all distant possessions must fall, let them be as valuable as their warmest panegyrists contend.

It evidently appears from this slight review of our most important dependencies, that on them we are not to exert that new policy which alone can be the preservation of the British power and consequence. The more important they are already, the less are they fit instruments in that work. No man can be hardy enough to deny that they are insecure; to add therefore to their value by exertions of policy which shall have the effect of directing any stream of capital, industry, or population into those channels, would be to add to a disproportion already an evil. The more we are convinced of the vast importance of those territories, the more we must feel the insecurity of our power; our view therefore ought not to be to increase but preserve them.

~ The British Monarchy website (http://www.royal.gov.uk)

I believe his letter candidly speaks to the realities of the British Empire crumbling beneath his feet. Britain would no longer be the superpower in trade and commerce. The disobedient children proved to their parents that they could make it on their own. The colonies were not the main source of British wealth but they were a large portion of it. The king underestimated his adversaries, thought they were a bunch of farmers with pitchforks, uneducated subjects revolting against him. Little did he know that the flame of freedom once ignited would never leave the land until the last soldier took his/her last breath.

Epilogue

History is mainly identified with war, diplomacy, and politics, all from which women were virtually excluded. Women are marginalized when it comes to writing about historical events. Traditional history obscured, abandoned, and misrepresented the historical record and experience of half the world's population, meaning women. I hope after reading this book you come to a new understanding that history was not taught to you properly. Historically, literature had been fundamentally monopolized by all-male universities and research institutes. This omission started to break down in the late nineteenth century worldwide. Consequently, including women in history may be tricky in dislodging or rectifying past distortions. However, it can be accomplished.

In America during the 1960s, a new history movement was born. Feminists noticed that women's perspectives, involvement, and culture were largely left out of history books. This movement was a demand to incorporate women into historical narratives. The 1960s was a tumultuous and decisive decade in American history. Martin Luther King and U.S. President John F. Kennedy were both assassinated, Americans feared the Cuban Missile Crisis (confrontation between the U.S. and the Soviet Union), civil unrest to end legalized racial discrimination, and equal rights for women. As a result of America's civil unrest and protests, America passed the Civil Rights Act of 1964.

The discipline of women's history did not begin until the 1970s. The goal of writing about the forgotten profiles of women who bravely fought in battles against Great Britain is to build a sound foundation so that women can truly be represented in historical literature about the American Revolutionary War. During the American Revolutionary War, women fought unconventionally against the British Empire. These women disguised themselves as men to become soldiers, became spies, delivered vital intelligence by being a courier, and in cases left their most precious possessions, their children, in the hands of friends and neighbors to fight against tyranny. Tyranny is when a person or a group of people or a régime has absolute power over citizens. These women knew that taking up arms against King George III would be automatic treason, and the punishment was death.

However, these women did not permit the fear of death to stop them from pursuing independence from an authoritarian regime. The number of women disguised as men and trained with their local militia may forever be a secret. In Colonial America, lower-class women were not permitted to be educated, thus causing the lack of heroines (many teenage women) writing down their own experiences on and off the battlefield.

Academia should not ignore or devalue these heroic women's actions. When historians and scholars fail to include females in combat roles during the American Revolutionary War, this manipulates historical information, which in turn retains the masculine identity of the Revolutionary War and strengthens control over marginalized groups such as women, all in the name of elevating men's roles versus women's accomplishments when fighting for America's freedom. Hegemonic structures underlie the systems we interact with every day, including the production and distribution of historical knowledge.[183] In the last half-century, historians finally started to pay attention to women in history and have tried to modify historical records such as revisions on legends, myths, and literature created by men regarding the representation of women. In the book *When We Dead Awaken: Writing as Re-Vision*, author Adrienne Rich asserts that revision—the act of looking back, of seeing with fresh eyes, of entering an old text from a new critical direction—is for women more than a chapter in cultural history: It is an act of survival.[184] In a book by Emily Werner titled *In Pursuit of Liberty: Coming of Age in the American Revolution*, she states that teenagers were a regular and much needed force because teenagers were invisible to adults and therefore extraordinarily little attention was paid to them. Werner also notes that one-third of the American population at the time of the Revolutionary War remained loyal to the British cause. Families were divided while Loyalist fathers sided with the British and their sons and daughters became Patriots. Women who broke the rules of social convention wanted to participate in creating a peaceful, accessible, and sustainable environment for all people in America.

Sadly, the sustainable environment these Patriots were fighting for happened decades later. The emancipation of slaves happened eighty years later (1863), and women did not become citizens or were viewed as semi-equal to men until 137 years later (the 1920s). Even though these women knew in their hearts of hearts that taking up arms against Great Britain might not guarantee their freedom, they still fought with the hope that it might happen. Ordinary citizens became Patriots and stood up against an oppressive government. While writing this book, I often wondered how many individuals in today's society would put down their iPhone to protest against a tyrannical government. Would they even notice? It seems around the world people are more interested in their virtual social bubble versus laws being passed that might infringe on their rights. Everyone should pay attention to what their government does. Just like Ronald Reagan said, *"Freedom is never more than one generation away from extinction."*

The qualitative research that I have proved is primary and secondary sources, which consisted of researching the National Archives, military correspondence letters, soldier journals, pension requests, newspaper articles published in the era of research, and firsthand documented testimonies. The evidence provided debunks any notion of these women being folklore and instead proves these women heroines, soldiers, and spies who did exist and performed extraordinary acts of heroism. Primary sources are as dependable as secondary sources and together create a reliable source. As we have learned and come to understand, a historian's job is to interpret the past factually without current fashionable political bias and who studies written records of history. The failure of academia in correcting the continuous historical errors of excluding courageous women who fought one way or another during the American Revolutionary War may reflect gender bias against women. This book educates and advocates for women to be incorporated in history as warriors, rather than history telling the story of their social class obligations and motherhood. If the women in this book were men, countless books would be written about them. Women are underrepresented when historical publications are concerned; history books are largely represented as male. All you have to do is go to a local library, pick up a history book involving the Revolutionary War, and you will not see anything mentioned about the women in this book. World-renowned authors of the 21st century still have yet to include these female warriors in their books. I hope that I am correcting that error.

In the field of history, several organizations have played critical roles in addressing gender bias. Rewriting history to project women's involvement is not impossible. However, many male historians would perceive adding women as a negative. Roman philosopher Marcus Tullius Cicero wrote that being ignorant of what occurred before birth is always a child. What is the worth of human life unless it is woven into the life of our ancestors by the records of history? History is not what happened but what human beings do to acquire reliable knowledge about what happened and how they convert such knowledge into an enlarged and enriched understanding of reality and their place in the world.[185] Put our women back in the history books!

Susan B. Anthony once said, *"There is not one foot of advance ground upon which women stand today that has not been obtained through the hard-fought battles of other women."* John Basil Barnhill, an anti-socialist writer, once stated in 1914, "When government fears the people, there is liberty. When the people fear the government, there is tyranny."[186]

Definitions of Terms

Acts – Taxes imposed by King George III and the Parliament of Great Britain believed they had a right to tax the colonies. So it was determined to reassert its authority in the Colonies by taxing his subjects to pay for the French and Indian War. The most significant acts (taxes) forced onto the thirteen colonies were the Stamp Act 1765, Quartering Act 1765, Declaratory Act 1766, Tea Act 1773, Townshend Act 1767, and Intolerable (Coercive) Act 1774.

Colonists – Are settlers whose ancestors colonized America, which was established some twenty years before, in 1587. British Colonists were members of the thirteen colonies.

Continental Army – After the battle of Lexington and Concord, the Second Continental Congress (1774 to 1789) created the Continental Army. General George Washington assumed command in 1775. Many of those enlisted were between the ages of fifteen and thirty.

Great Britain Parliament – Parliament is made up of three central elements: the House of Commons, the House of Lords and the Monarchy[187] (at the time of the Revolutionary War, it was King George III). Parliament continues to be the supreme legal authority of Britain. During the Revolution year they forced overreaching taxation measures against the American colonies in the late 1760s.

Indentured Servant – A person who signs and is bound by indentures to work for another for a specified time, especially in return for payment of travel expenses and maintenance.

Loyalist – A British subject who remained loyal to Great Britain and King George III and was opposed by the Patriots. Loyalists were also called Tories, King's Men, and Royalists.

Militia – Are male civilian colonists who independently organized regiments to train in weaponry, military tactics and strategies. All able-bodied men were required to serve. Some colonies' age requirements were between sixteen and sixty.

Patriots – Were British colonists who rejected British Tyranny, who desired independence and the freedom to govern themselves. Patriots are also known as Revolutionaries, Rebels, Continentals, and American Whigs.

Natives – Are tribes of people who are estimated to inhabit America around B.C. 8000–1000. It is believed these natives came across the land bridge from Asia. Also known to Americans as Native Indians or Native Americans.

Thirteen Colonies – Were colonies from Great Britain located on the Atlantic coast of America. Those colonies were Connecticut, Delaware, Georgia, Maryland, Massachusetts, New Hampshire, New Jersey, New York, Pennsylvania, North Carolina, Rhode Island, South Carolina, and Virginia.

Revolutionary War – Colonists waged a full-scale war for independence against overreach by King George II of Great Britain. The Lexington and Concord battles between British troops and Colonial militiamen in April 1775 kicked off the armed conflict.

Slaves – A person who is forced to work for and obey another and is considered to be their property; an enslaved person.

Tories – A person loyal to Britain and the King of Britain.

Endnotes

[1] Wood, W.; and A. H. Eagly. *"A cross-cultural analysis of the behavior of women and men: Implications for the origins of sex differences."* Psychological Bulletin, 128 (5) (2002), pp. 699-727, 10.1037/0033-2909.128.5.699.

[2] Asian history. Asian History, 31 May 2011, https://asianhistory.tumblr.com/post/6035871160/folk-art-of-trieu-thi-trinh-depicted-as-a.

[3] *"World Eras. Encyclopedia.com. 24 Jan. 2022."* Encyclopedia.com, Encyclopedia.com, 14 Feb. 2022, https://www.encyclopedia.com/history/news-wires-white-papers-and-books/queen-amina.

[4] Ibid

[5] "Facts about the Continental Army during the American Revolution." Boston Tea Party Ships, 21 June 2021,https://www.bostonteapartyship.com/facts-continental-army#:~:text=Soldiers%20were%20promised%20a%20pay,of%20liberty%20despite%20the%20hardships.

[6] *"Women in the United States Army."* Women in the U.S. Army | The United States Army, https://www.army.mil/women/history/.

[7] DE PAUW, LINDA GRANT. *"Women in Combat: THE REVOLUTIONARY WAR EXPERIENCE."* Armed Forces & Society, vol. 7, no. 2, 1981, pp. 209–26. JSTOR, http://www.jstor.org/stable/45346224. Accessed 21 Jul. 2022.

[8] Ibid

[9] Great man theory, Wikipedia

[10] "Great Man Theory of Leadership." Great Man Theory of Leadership, https://www.managementstudyguide.com/great-man-theory.htm.

[11] Garrison, Arthur. "The Rule Of Law And The Rise Of Control Of Executive Power." Texas Review of Law & Politics, vol. 18, no. 2, University of Texas, Austin, School of Law Publications, Inc., Apr. 2014, p. 303.

[12] A famous quote by Rosa Parks is *"one person can change the world."* 1950s

[13] Bohrer, Melissa Lukeman. *"Glory, Passion, and Principle: The Story of Eight Remarkable Women at the Core of the American Revolution."* Atria Books, 2004.

[14] Rich, Adrienne. *"When We Dead Awaken: Writing as Re-Vision."* College English, vol. 34, no. 1, National Council of Teachers of English, 1972, pp. 18–30, https://doi.org/10.2307/375215.

[15] Fiske, John. *"The American Revolution."* Vol I&II, Houghton, Mifflin & CO., 1896.

[16] McCullough, David. *"1776."* Allen Lane/Penguin Books, 2005.

[17] Hall, Brianna, et al. *"Great Women of the American Revolution."* Capstone Press, 2013.

[18] Morgan, Robin. *"Sisterhood Is Powerful: An Anthology of Writings from the Women's Liberation Movement."* Vintage Books, 1970.

[19] Shayne, Julie. *"Introduction: Fifty Years of Women's Studies."* Persistence Is Resistance Celebrating 50 Years of Gender Women Sexuality Studies, University of Washington Libraries, 12 Aug. 2020, https://uw.pressbooks.pub/happy50thws/chapter/introduction-fifty-years-of-womens-studies/#:~:text=Women's%20Studies%2C%20as%20a%20distinct,al%2C%20this%20collection.).

[20] Guy-Sheftall, Beverly. "Women's Studies Scholarship: Its Impact on the Information World." Social Responsibilities Round Tables, 16 Aug. 2019, https://www.ala.org/rt/srrt/feminist-task-force/womens-studies-scholarship-impact.

[21] A. Chick, Kay. (2006). Gender Balance in K-12 American History Textbooks. Social Studies Research and Practice. https://www.womenshistory.org/sites/default/files/museum-assets/document/2018-01/NWHM_Status-of-Women-in-State-Social-Studies-Standards.pdf

[22] Magazine, Smithsonian. *"What Schools Teach about Women's History Leaves a Lot to Be Desired."* Smithsonian.com, Smithsonian Institution, 1 Mar. 2019, https://www.smithsonianmag.com/history/what-schools-teach-womens-history-180971447/.

[23] Grenier, John. The First Way of War: American War Making on the Frontier, 1607-1814. E-book, Cambridge [U.K.]: Cambridge University Press, 2005, https://hdl-handle-net.ezproxy1.apus.edu/2027/heb.31589. Accessed 17 Apr 2020.

[24] The phrase is attributed to James Otis, which reflected the resentment of colonists being taxed by the British Parliament, to which they elected no representatives and became an anti-British slogan.

[25] Library of Congress. *The Library of Congress*, 2009, www.loc.gov/collections/Continental-congress-and-constitutional-convention-from-1774-to-1789/articles-and-essays/timeline/1766-to-1767/.

[26] A proclamation would permit the military to pursue more aggressive measures against the colonists and punish supporters who support the cause of independence from Great Britain.

[27] Treaty of Paris, History.com https://www.history.com/topics/american-revolution/treaty-of-paris

[28] Treaty of Paris, 1783. U.S. Department of State, U.S. Department of State, 2005, https://2001-2009.state.gov/r/pa/ho/time/ar/14313.htm.

[29] David Ammerman: *"The British Constitution and the American Revolution: A Failure of Precedent."* William & Mary Law Review, March 1976.

[30] Website Colonial Williamsburg https://www.history.org/history/teaching/tchcrone.cfm

[31] History.com, Tea Act, September 25, 2019

[32] "The Declaratory Act." *The Colonial Williamsburg Foundation*, 2021, http://ouramericanrevolution.org/index.cfm/page/view/p0062.

[33] Benjamin Franklin was a statesman and political activist for the colonies. Who signed all three documents (the Declaration of Independence, Treaty of Paris, and the U.S. Constitution) which freed the colonies from Great Britain's iron fist.

[34] History.com Editors. "Tea Act." History.com, A&E Television Networks, 9 Nov. 2009, https://www.history.com/topics/american-revolution/tea-act.

[35] Declaration of Independence – Par Two (*The Grievances*) https://www.dentonisd.org/cms/lib/tx21000245/centricity/domain/4034/declaration%20of%20independence%20activity%20part%20ii-%20preap.pdf

[36] Smith, Michael W. *"The Sacrifices Made by the Declaration Signers"* Michael W. Smith, 2021, https://michaelwsmith.com/the-sacrifices-made-by-the-declaration-signers/.

[37] Nuwer, Rachel. "Brits Have Invaded Nine out of Ten Countries." Smithsonian.com, Smithsonian Institution, 5 Nov. 2012, https://www.smithsonianmag.com/smart-news/brits-have-invaded-nine-out-of-ten-countries-109283469/.

[38] "[Colonial Period]. A Group of 4 Colonial American Newspapers. 1768-1772." *[COLONIAL PERIOD]. A Group of 4 Colonial American Newspapers. 1768-1772. | Cowan's Auction House: The Midwest's Most Trusted Auction House / Antiques / Fine Art / Art Appraisals*, The Boston Chronicle, 2000, https://www.cowanauctions.com/lot/Colonial-period-a-group-of-4-Colonial-american-newspapers-1768-1772-4090923.

[39] Stewart, Richard W. "*THE UNITED STATES ARMY AND THE FORGING OF A NATION, 1775-1917.*" Chapter 3: American Military History, Volume I, Center of Military History United States Army, 2005, history.army.mil/books/AMH-V1/ch03.htm.

[40] Office of the Historian website. https://history.state.gov/milestones/1776-1783/french-alliance

[41] Teaching History website. https://teachinghistory.org/history-content/ask-a-historian/22894

[42] The National Library of the Netherlands website. https://geheugen.delpher.nl/en/geheugen/pages/collectie/Atlantic+World/De+Nederlandse+betrokkenheid+bij+de+Amerikaanse+Onafhankelijkheidsoorlog

[43] Barker, H., & Chalus, E. (1997). "*Gender in Eighteenth-Century England: Roles, Representations and Responsibilities*" (1st ed.). Routledge. https://doi.org/10.4324/9781315842523

[44] Boundless US History. Lumen, https://courses.lumenlearning.com/boundless-ushistory/chapter/the-role-of-women-in-the-colonies/.

45 Wahrman, Dror. *"Varieties of Gender in Eighteenth-Century England."* The Making of the Modern Self, Yale University Press, 2017, pp. 7–44, https://doi.org/10.12987/9780300134599-005.

46 Mays, Dorothy A. and ABC-Clio Information Services. Women in Early America. (Santa Barbara, Calif.: Abc-Clio, 2004.); 137.

47 John Brown, *An Estimate on the Manners and Principles of the Times*. L. Davis, and C. Reymers, in Holborn; printers to the Royal Society, Oxford University, 1757, p. 51.

48 Bethke-Elshtain, Jean *"Feminism's Search for Politics, in Public Man, Private Women: Women in Social and Political Thought, "* Princeton, N.J., and Oxford University, 1981, pg. 202-97 provides a detailed and accessible examination of the similarities and differences among racial, liberal, Marxist, and psychoanalytic feminisms.

49 Sanders, Kevin. *"Why Were Women Written out of History? An Interview with Bettany Hughes."* English Heritage Blog, English Heritage, 28 Feb. 2017, blog.english-heritage.org.uk/women-written-history-interview-bettany-hughes/.

50 Ibid

51 Poniewozik, James. Books: *"Timeline"* By Michael Crichton." Time (Chicago, Ill.), vol. 154, no. 21, Time, Inc, 1999.

52 *The Fighting Man of the Continental Army.* https://www.battlefields.org/learn/articles/fighting-man-Continental-army

53 *"To John Adams from William Tudor, 6 September 1776,"* Founders Online, National Archives, https://founders.archives.gov/documents/Adams/06-05-02-0007. Original source: *The Adams Papers, Papers of John Adams*, vol. 5, August 1776–March 1778, ed. Robert J. Taylor. Cambridge, MA: Harvard University Press, 2006, pp. 13–15.

54 Leahy, Ethel, 1931, "*Who's Who on the Ohio River and its Tributaries*"

55 Lawrence J. Fleenor, Jr. "*The History of Yellow Creek*". Archived from the original on 2007-09-01.

56 *Sketches of History, Life, and Manners, in the United States*. By a Traveler. Ohio: Printed for the author, 1826, 1963.

57 U.S. Compiled Revolutionary War Military Service Records, 1775-1783 [database on-line]. Provo, UT, USA: Operations Inc, 2010.

58 Professor of history at the University of Richmond and author of several books including *The American Revolution, Nationhood Archives 1763 to 1788,* and *George Washington's enforcers; policing the Continental Army*.

59 U.S. Compiled Revolutionary War Military Service Records, 1775-1783 [database on-line]. New Hampshire: Reed's Regiment

60 "*George Washington and the Final British Campaign for the Hudson River, 1779*." Reference and Research Book News, vol. 27, no. 5, 2012. ProQuest, https://www.proquest.com/trade-journals/george-washington-final-british-campaign-hudson/docview/1081889943/se-2?accountid=8289.

61 "*The German Battalion*." German Marylanders, https://www.germanmarylanders.org/profile-index/military/the-german-battalion.

62 Perreira, Julian. "*Bayonet Fighting: All of the General*" Forces Network, 9 Feb. 2021, https://www.forces.net/feature/bayonet-fighting-all-gen#:~:text=It%20is%20the%20weapon%20of,confined%20spaces%20or%20cle aring%20trenches.

63 "*The Battle of Princeton | Princeton Alumni Weekly*." Princeton University, The Trustees of Princeton University, https://paw.princeton.edu/article/battle-princeton.

[64] *"Battle of Germantown."* Encyclopedia Britannica, Encyclopedia Britannica, Inc., https://www.britannica.com/event/Battle-of-Germantown.

[65] Ibid

[66] Cridlin, William Broaddus. 4 Nov 1923, 67 – *"The Times Dispatch"* at Newspapers.com." Newspapers.com, 2005, https://www.newspapers.com/image/616145144/?terms=State+Pensioned+Brave+Girl+Who+Fought+As+Man+Until+severely+Wounded+at+Germantown+Battl e&match=1.

[67] *"British Abandon Philadelphia."* History.com, A&EE Television Networks, 13 Nov. 2009, https://www.history.com/this-day-in-history/british-abandon-philadelphia.

[68] *"George Washington to Israel Putnam, September 14, 1777."* The Library of Congress, https://www.loc.gov/resource/mgw3b.004/?sp=115. George Washington Papers: Series 3, Varick Transcripts, 1775 to 1785 (44)

[69] Aron, Paul. "*Fighting as a Common Soldier.*" Colonial Williamsburg Wax Seal, 20 Oct. 2020, https://orgcmsprod.cwf.org/trend-tradition-magazine/spring-2017/fighting-common-soldier/.

[70] *"Anna Maria Lane Chapter, NSDAR SWEA City, Iowa."* Daughters of the American Revolution, 29 Nov. 2020, http://www.isdar.org/chapters/annamarialane/Anna_Maria_Lane_biography.html.

[71] Letter, William H. Cabell to Speaker of the House of Delegates. 28 January 1808. Manuscript. RG 3, Governor's Office, Executive Letter Books, William H. Cabell, 8 July 1807–9 March 1808. Acc. 35358, The Library of Virginia. https://www.lva.virginia.gov/exhibits/destiny/where_women/cabell.htm. [Accessed 05 June 2020].

[72] Aron, Paul. "*Fighting as a Common Soldier*." Colonial Williamsburg Wax Seal, 20 Oct. 2020, https://orgcmsprod.cwf.org/trend-tradition-magazine/spring-2017/fighting-common-soldier/.

[73] Anne Waller Reddy, application for Headstone, dated 1936.Findagrave.com

[74] Treadway, Sandra Gioia. "*Anna Maria Lane: An Uncommon Soldier of the American Revolution*." Virginia Cavalcade 37, no. 3 (1988): 134–143. Danyluk, Kaia K. "*Women and the Revolutionary War*." Colonial Williamsburg Interpreter (Fall 1997): 8–13.

[75] Berkin, Carol. "*Revolutionary Mothers: Women in the Struggle for America's Independence*." Knopf, 2005.

[76] U.S. Sons of the American Revolution Membership applications, 1889-1970. SAR membership #: 78560

[77] Walker, Melissa A. "*The Battles of Kings Mountain and Cowpens: The American Revolution in the Southern Backcountry*," Taylor & Francis Group, 2012. ProQuest E-book Central, https://ebookcentral.proquest.com/lib/apus/detail.action?docID=1125214.

[78] Brady Dearden. "*A LEGACY OF PRINCIPLES AND LEADERSHIP: DECISIVE VICTORY AT COWPENS*." Infantry (Online), vol. 105, no. 2, Infantry Magazine, 2016, p. 70– 15 Oct. 2020.

[79] Ibid.

[80] "*Daniel Morgan*." National Parks Service, U.S. Department of the Interior, https://www.nps.gov/cowp/learn/historyculture/daniel-morgan.htm.

[81] Ibid

82 *"Battle of Cowpens."* George Washington's Mount Vernon, https://www.mountvernon.org/library/digitalhistory/digital-encyclopedia/article/battle-of-cowpens/.

83 Ancestry.com. U.S., Sons of the American Revolution Membership Applications, 1889-1970 [database on-line]. Provo, UT, USA: Ancestry.com Operations, Inc., 10 Oct. 2020.

84 *"Battle of Cowpens."* George Washington's Mount Vernon, https://www.mountvernon.org/library/digitalhistory/digital-encyclopedia/article/battle-of-cowpens/.

85 *"Margaret 'Peggy' Moore Barry (1752-1823)."* Find a Grave, 9 Oct. 2011, https://www.findagrave.com/memorial/78000831/margaret-catherine-barry.

86 Pepperell Historical Commission . Pepperell Town Clerk's Records, Nov. 2, 1858, Vol. 5, page 232. https://town.pepperell.ma.us/160/Covered-Bridge-Over-the-Nashua-River [Accessed 10 July 2020].

87 Prudence Cummings Wright, Patriot Militia Commander, Captures 2 British Spies. New England Historical Society. https://www.newenglandhistoricalsociety.com/prudence-cummings-wright-Patriot-militia-commander-captures-2-british-spies/ . [Accessed 09 July 2020].

88 Prudence Wright Memorial Stone. https://town.pepperell.ma.us/gallery.aspx?PID=70. [Accessed 09 July 2020].

89 True Stories of the Days of Washington. N.p., n.p., 1861.

90 https://www.carolana.com/SC/Revolution/revolution_sc_second_regiment.html

91 Gray, Jefferson (Autumn 2011). *"Up from the swamp: Francis Marion turned South Carolina's Low Country into a quagmire for the British and became one of history's greatest guerrilla leaders"*. MHQ: The Quarterly Journal of Military History. 24 (1): 56–65.

92 Willett, Edward. Julia Bartram, Or, the Swamp Scouts: *A Tale of Marion's Men*. United States, American News Company, publishers' agent, 1866.

93 *"Wadboo Barony: Francis Marion's Last Headquarters Historical Marker."* *Historical Marker*, The Historical Marker Database, 16 June 2016, https://www.hmdb.org/m.asp?m=53891.

94 James William Dobein. *A Sketch of the Life of Brig. General Francis Marion.* Project Gutenberg 1997. INSERT-MISSING-DATABASE-NAME http://search.ebscohost.com/login.aspx?direct=true&scope=site&db=nlebk&db=nlabk&AN=1029800.

95 Bid

96 Berkin, Carol (2007). *Revolutionary Mothers: Women in the Struggle for America's Independence.* Knopf Doubleday Publishing Group. p. 61. ISBN 9780307427496.

97 "Camp Followers." *George Washington's Mount Vernon*, 2008, https://www.mountvernon.org/library/digitalhistory/digital-encyclopedia/article/camp-followers/. camp followers in New York, women retained as cooks received the same wages as men in that position.1 In rare cases, women assumed combat roles equal to those of their husbands. Mary Ludwig Hayes (memorialized as "Molly Pitcher"), Margaret Corbin, and Anna Maria Lane are all examples of women who demonstrated their Patriotism by joining men in battle.

98 Brooks, Rebecca Beatrice. *"The Roles of Women in the Revolutionary War."* History of Massachusetts Blog, History of Massachusetts, 7 Feb. 2013, https://historyofmassachusetts.org/the-roles-of-women-in-the-revolutionary-war/.

[99] General Orders, 4 August 1777, *Founders Online, National Archives*, https://founders.archives.gov/documents/Washington/03-10-02-0508. [Original source: *The Papers of George Washington, Revolutionary War Series*, vol. 10, 11 June 1777–18 August 1777, ed. Frank E. Grizzard, Jr. Charlottesville: University Press of Virginia, 2000, pp. 496–497.]

[100] Pittman, Katharine. "*5 Things You Might Not Have Known about Martha Washington.*" Colonial Williamsburg, https://www.colonialwilliamsburg.org/learn/living-history/5-things-you-might-not-have-known-about-martha-washington/#:~:text=4.,Chief%20of%20the%20Continental%20Army.

[101] United States Continental Congress, *Journals of the Continental Congress*, 1774-1789. Edited from the original record in the Library of Congress Washington, U.S. Govt. print off., 1904-37. 34 v. front. (v.9) facsims. (part fold.) 27 cm. KF4505.U55 1904, https://lccn.loc.gov/05000059.

[102] Ibid

[103] "*Americans at War.*" Encyclopedia.com. 25 Jan. 2022." Encyclopedia.com, Encyclopedia.com, https://www.encyclopedia.com/defense/energy-government-and-defense-magazines/camp-followers-war-and-women.

[104] Jesse. "*The Importance of Army 'Camp Followers' before Modern Day Military Logistics.*" WAR HISTORY ONLINE, https://www.warhistoryonline.com/war-articles/followers.html.

[105] "*Molly Pitcher Folklore. Daughters of the American Revolution*", https://www.members.dar.org/national-society/molly-pitcher-folklore.

[106] Ratcliffe, Christine Celano. "*First Women Nurses.*" History of American Women, https://www.womenhistoryblog.com/2014/07/first-women-nurses.html.

107 Brooks, Rebecca Beatrice. *"The Roles of Women in the Revolutionary War."* History of Massachusetts, Blog, History of Massachusetts, https://historyofmassachusetts.org/the-roles-of-women-in-the-revolutionary-war/.

108 Emma Ward. *"Ladylike: The Necessity and Neglect of Camp Followers in the Continental Army"* Western Kentucky University, https://digitalcommons.wku.edu/cgi/viewcontent.cgi?article=1923&context =stu_hon_theses.

109 Teipe, Emily J. *"Will the Real Molly Pitcher Please Stand up?"* National Archives and Records Administration, National Archives and Records Administration, 1999, https://www.archives.gov/publications/prologue/1999/summer/pitcher.html.

110 Ibid

111 Hannah Winthrop to Mercy Otis Warren, Nov. 11, 1777, in Massachusetts Historical Society Collections 73 (1925), vol. 2, pp. 451–453.

112 American Revolutionary War museum, Camp Follower, https://www.amrevmuseum.org/virtualexhibits/picturing-washington-s-army/pages/campfollowers

113 Ancestry.com, Margaret Corbin in the U.S., Find A Grave Index, 1600s-Current. https://search.ancestry.com/cgi-

114 Michals, Debra. *"Margaret Cochran Corbin."* National Women's History Museum. 2015. www.womenshistory.org/education-resources/biographies/margaret-cochran-corbin.

115 Michals, Debra. *"Margaret Cochran Corbin."* National Women's History Museum, https://www.womenshistory.org/education-resources/biographies/margaret-cochran-corbin.

[116] Michals, Debra. "*Margaret Cochran Corbin.*" National Women's History Museum. 2015. www.womenshistory.org/education-resources/biographies/margaret-cochran-corbin.

[117] "*British Forces Defeat Patriots in the Battle of Brooklyn.*" History.com, A&E Television Networks, 21 July 2010, https://www.history.com/this-day-in-history/the-battle-of-brooklyn#:~:text=Howe%20failed%20to%20follow%20the,the%20Continental%20Army%20from%20capture.

[118] Teipe, Emily. "*Will the Real Molly Pitcher Please Stand up?*" Prologue Magazine. National Archives. Vol. 31, No. 2, 1999. https://www.archives.gov/publications/prologue/1999/summer/pitcher.html

[119] Michals, Debra. "*Margaret Cochran Corbin.*" National Women's History Museum, https://www.womenshistory.org/education-resources/biographies/margaret-cochran-corbin.

[120] Price, William. "*Report from West Point.*" Papers of the War Department · Report from West Point · Papers of the War Department, https://wardepartmentpapers.org/s/home/item/37682.

[121] Journal of the Continental Congress, 1774-1789, Vol 14, page 805. https://memory.loc.gov/cgi-bin/query/r?ammem/hlaw:@field(DOCID+@lit(jc01464))

[122] Continental Congress, Journals of the Continental Congress, 1774–1789, micro card editions, 1975, p. 805. The "*One-half of a monthly salary drawn by a soldier*" (i.e., a private) amounted to less than two dollars a month. Allen Bowman, The Morale of the American Revolutionary Army (1964), pp. 23–24, explains the difficulty in assessing wages. Initially, a private's monthly salary was $6.66, which was reduced by twenty-five percent early in the war. Corbin's disability pay was probably about two dollars a month.

[123] Library of Congress. "*Journals of the Continental Congress, 1774-1789.*" American Memory: Remaining Collections, LIBRARY OF CONGRESS, memory.loc.gov/cgi-

bin/query/r?ammem%2Fhlaw%3A%40field%28DOCID%2B%40lit%28jc01464%29%29.

[124] "*Margaret Corbin.*" History of American Women, 2 Apr. 2017, https://www.womenhistoryblog.com/2010/05/margaret-corbin.html.

[125] Field Book of the Revolution" (Harper Bros., 1855) should be of interest to all American Field Artillerymen

[126] Joseph Plumb Martin, *A Narrative of Some of the Adventures, Dangers, and Sufferings of a Revolutionary Soldier,* Hallowell, Maine, 1830), 96-97.

[127] Fredriksen, John. "*Mary Ludwig Hays (1754-1832).*" *What Happened?:* An Encyclopedia of Events That Changed America Forever, vol. 2, 2011, pp. 202–03.

[128] Pension Application of Aaron Osborn, w4558

[129] Pentecost, Corinne. "8 Jul 1956, 1 - Scrantonian Tribune at Newspapers.com." Newspapers.com, https://www.newspapers.com/image/530273111/?terms=Sarah+Benjamin& match=1.

[130] National Archives, 20 Nov. 2019, https://todaysdocument.tumblr.com/post/189189096433/sarah-benjamins-eyewitness-account-of-the.

[131] Sarah Osborn is one of the pensioners featured in John C. Dann, *The Revolution Remembered* (1980), pp. 240–250. Dann states that she received a double pension based upon the service of both veteran husbands. However, John Benjamin's pension card file indicates that she was pensioned as the former widow of Aaron Osborn of New York. There is no mention of any widow's benefits under Benjamin. Her complete application is filed under Osborn's name. She states in her affidavit that Aaron Osborn later sold the bounty land of 160 acres that he had received to pay some debts. In 1837 she claimed to be eighty-one. If that was her correct age, then she was 108 years old when she died in 1864.

[132] World History Project.org, *1774, Paul Revere Becomes A Member of The First Patriot Intelligence Network, 'The Mechanics,* 2022

[133] Founders Online: "To George Washington from John Jay, 19 November 1778." *National Archives and Records Administration*, National Archives and Records Administration, 2008, founders.archives.gov/documents/Washington/03-18-02-0218.

[134] DeWan, George. "*The Mystery of Agent 355.*" Newsday, Newsday, 2 June 2014, www.newsday.com/long-island/history/the-mystery-of-agent-355-unraveling-the-case-of-the-Patriot-spy-who-never-was-1.7512149.

[135] History.com Editors. "*The HMS New Jersey.*" History.com, A&E Television Networks, 19 Mar. 2010, www.history.com/topics/american-revolution/the-hms-jersey#:~:text=The%20most%20infamous%20British%20prison,as%20from%20the%20effects%20of .

[136] Booth, Sally Smith. "*The Women of '76.*" Hastings House, 1976.

[137] Bohrer, Melissa Lukeman. "*Glory, Passion, and Principle: The Story of Eight Remarkable Women at the Core of the American Revolution.*" Atria Books, 2004.

[138] Lineage Book, *Daughters of the American Revolution*, Vol. 69, p. 350.

139 The National Archives; Washington, D.C.; Ledgers of Payments, 1818-1872, to U.S. Pensioners Under Acts of 1818 Through 1858 From Records of the Office of the Third Auditor of the Treasury; Record Group Title: Records of the Accounting Officers of the Department of the Treasury; Record Group Number: 217; Series Number: T718; Roll Number: 18

140 Judith Mower Goodman, *"History of the Blair Family"* (Blair genealogy file, Quaker Collection, Guilford College, Greensboro).

141 DAR Oregon State Roster of Ancestors, 1963

142 Find a Grave https://www.findagrave.com/memorial/16032709/hannah-millikan-blair

143 Michals, Debra. *"Lydia Barrington Darragh."* National Women's History Museum. National Women's History Museum, 2015. March 26, 2021.

144 History.com Editors. *"Philadelphia Nurse Overhears British Plans to Attack Washington's Army."* History.com, A&E Television Networks, 13 Nov. 2009, www.history.com/this-day-in-history/philadelphia-nurse-overhears-british-plans-to-attack-washington.

145 To George Washington from William Dewees, Jr., 4 December 1777," Founders Online, National Archives, https://founders.archives.gov/documents/Washington/03-12-02-0496. [Original source: The Papers of George Washington, Revolutionary War Series, vol. 12, 26 October 1777–25 December 1777, ed. Frank E. Grizzard, Jr. and David R. Hoth. Charlottesville: University Press of Virginia, 2002, pp. 538–541.]

146 American Quarterly Review, *"American Biography"* Vol. I. pp. 32-34 (1827)

147 Bohrer, Melissa Lukeman. *"Glory, Passion, and Principle: The Story of Eight Remarkable Women at the Core of the American Revolution."* Atria Books, 2004.

148 American Battlefield Trust *"Lydia Barrington Darragh - Patriot Spy."* 5 Mar. 2019, www.battlefields.org/learn/biographies/lydia-barrington-darragh.

149 U.S. Sons of the American Revolution Membership Applications, 1889-1970

150 Georgia Historic Newspapers. *Savannah Republican.* (Savannah, Ga.) 1824-1829, October 06, 1825, Image 2 " Georgia Historic Newspapers, 2021, gahistoricnewspapers.galileo.usg.edu/lccn/sn87062327/1825-10-06/ed-1/seq-2/#sort=date_asc&index=8&rows=12&proxtext=Nancy+Hart&sequence=0&words=HART+Hart+Nancy+NANCY&page=1.

151 The Atlantic Constitution Newspaper, https://www.newspapers.com/newspage/34099642/ December 23, 1912. *"Skeletons of Six Tories Hanged near Elberton, Found. "* (page 3)

152 "Heroine." Merriam-Webster, Merriam-Webster, 1999, https://www.merriam-webster.com/dictionary/heroine.

153 https://www.knowitall.org/video/emily-geiger-idella-bodies-sc-women-full-version

154 Chapman, John A. *"Chapman's History of South Carolina."* Emily Geiger, Chapter XXVIII, Pages 134, 135, 136, 137, Everett Waddey Co, 1897.

155 McC. Legare, Harriette. *"Proof of the Ride Taken by Emily Geiger During the American Revolution, and Also Proof of Her Existence."* Emily Geiger Affidavits, State of South Carolina, 2000, https://sciway3.net/clark/revolutionarywar/geiger16.html.

156 Enclosure: Elizabeth Burgin to James Caldwell, 19 November 1779," Founders Online, National Archives, https://founders.archives.gov/documents/Washington/03-23-02-0550-0002. [Original source: The Papers of George Washington, Revolutionary War Series, vol. 23, 22 October–31 December 1779, ed. William M. Ferraro. Charlottesville: University of Virginia Press, 2015, pp. 717–719.]

157 Journal of the American Revolution, Elizabeth Burgin Helps the Prisoners…
Somehow, September 11, 2014

158 Worthington Chauncey Ford et al., eds. Journals of the Continental Congress,
1774-1789. 34 vols

159 https://catalog.archives.gov/id/5913711

160 "*From George Washington to Samuel Huntington, 25 December 1779,*"
Founders Online, National Archives,
https://founders.archives.gov/documents/Washington/03-23-02-0550-0001-0001.
[Original source: The Papers of George Washington, Revolutionary War Series,
vol. 23, 22 October–31 December 1779, ed. William M. Ferraro. Charlottesville:
University of Virginia Press, 2015, pp. 715–717.]

161 Elizabeth Burgin to Reverend James Calville, 19 November 1779, Papers of
the Continental Congress, National Archives, Washington, DC. Images of the
manuscript are on line at: http://research.archives.gov/description/5916026

162 Wolf, Mark. "*Patriot Siege of Ninety-Six Ninety-Six, South Carolina, Begins.*"
Minuteman Militia, 22 May 2017, minuteman-militia.com/2017/05/22/Patriot-
siege-ninety-six-south-carolina-begins/.

163 Hanaford, Phebe, "*Daughters of American,*" Women of the Century, True and
company. 1883, pg. 179

164 The Portland transcript, v. XIX, no. 30, Saturday, Nov. 3, 1855

165 Cornwell, Ilene J. "*Three South Carolina Sites Associated with Revolutionary
"Feminist" Jane Black Thomas* (1720-1811)," Greeneville Magazine, 1986,
www.sciway3.net/clark/revolutionarywar/JaneBlackThomas.htm.

166 Logan John: "*The Part Taken by Women in American History*" Published by
The Perry-Nalle Publishing Company, Wilmington, Delaware, 1912.

167 Backett, Jennifer. *"Defending with a Sward - Jane Black."* Ancestry, 19 June 2017, www.ancestry.com/mediaui-viewer/tree/101501230/person/200098940074/media/9a21e22d-23c5-491d-a9ae-f4ecb3df7498?_phsrc=lhk1498&_phstart=successSource.

168 https://www.wikitree.com/wiki/Aldis-23#_note-1

169 Find a Grave Memorial ID: 121562069

170 Logan, Mary Simmerson Cunningham *"The part taken by women in American history"* Wilmington, Del., Perry-Nalle Pub. Co., 1912

171 DeHass, Wills. *"History of the Early Settlement and Indian Wars of Western Virginia."* Internet Archive, Wheeling, H. Hoblitzell; Philadelphia, Printed by King & Baird, 1 Jan. 1970, https://archive.org/details/historyofearlyse00deha/page/n8/mode/2up.

172 The Macon Telegraph (Macon, Georgia), April 13, 1917.

173 The Alabama, U.S., Surname Files Expanded, 1702–1981

174 Waters, Philemon Berry, Herbert M. Milam, and South Carolina Historical Society. A Genealogical History of the Waters and Kindred Families: In Two Parts. Atlanta, Georgia: Foote & Davies Company, 1902. https://archive.org/details/agenealogicalhi00socigoog/page/n14

175 This imitation of Longfellow's well-known ballad first appeared in The Sunday Star: This Week's Magazine, Washington, O. C, April 14, 1940. It is reprinted in Sybil Ludington: A Call to Anns by V. T. Dacquino which is reviewed in this issue of HVRR.

176 Smith, David. *"Why the British Were Doomed from the Get-Go in the American Revolutionary War."* LiveScience. History of War magazine, July 1, 2020. https://www.livescience.com/british-strategy-failure-during-american-revolution.html.

[177] Scott Rank. *"Revolutionary War Battles in South Carolina."* History of the Net, October 15, 2019. https://www.historyonthenet.com/revolutionary-war-battles-in-south-carolina.

[178] Dearden, Brady. *"A LEGACY OF PRINCIPLES AND LEADERSHIP: DECISIVE VICTORY AT COWPENS."* Infantry (Online) 105.2 (2016): 70-6. ProQuest. 30 Dec. 2020.

[179] Dearden, Brady. *"A LEGACY OF PRINCIPLES AND LEADERSHIP: DECISIVE VICTORY AT COWPENS."* Infantry (Online) 105.2 (2016): 70-6. ProQuest. 31 Dec. 2020.

[180] O'Shaughnessy, Andrew J. T*he Men Who Lost America: British Leadership, the American Revolution, and the Fate of the Empire*, Yale University Press, 2013. ProQuest E-book Central, https://ebookcentral.proquest.com/lib/apus/detail.action?docID=3421249.

[181] Jacobsen, Kristin. *"Master of Military Art and Science Theses."* Ike Skelton Combined Arms Research Library (CARL) Digital Library. University of Rhode Island, 1999. https://cgsc.contentdm.oclc.org/digital/collection/p4013coll2/id/74.

[182] Stewart, Richard W. *"THE UNITED STATES ARMY AND THE FORGING OF A NATION, 1775-1917."* Chapter 3: American Military History, Volume I, Center of Military History United States Army, 2005, history.army.mil/books/AMH-V1/ch03.htm.

[183] Shannon, Hope. *"What Does 'Lost' History Really Mean?"* Omnia History, 8 May 2019, https://omniahistory.com/2018/09/what-does-lost-history-really-mean/.

[184] Rich, Adrienne. *"When We Dead Awaken: Writing as Re-Vision."* College English, vol. 34, no. 1, National Council of Teachers of English, 1972, pp. 18–30, https://doi.org/10.2307/375215.

[185] Pamela S. Hinds, Doris E. Chaves and Sandra M. Cypess, Context as a Source of *Meaning and Understanding, Qualitative Health Research,* 10.1177/104973239200200105, 2, 1, (61-74), (2016).

[186] John Basil Barnhill, ***Barnhill-Tichenor Debate on Socialism, As It Appeared in the National Rip-Saw*** (Saint Louis, Mo.: The National Rip-Saw Pub. Co., 1914), 34.

[187] What is the role of Parliament – UK Parliament https://www.Parliament.uk/about/how/role/